DEPARTMENT OF DEFENSE
DEFENSE SUPPLY AGENCY

SALE NO. 16–5049

BID OPENING:
30 APRIL 1975 – 2:00 P.M.

SEALED BID

Offering...

HEAVY CRUISER
EX–CA–135

GUIDED MISSILE LIGHT CRUISER
EX–CLG–3

(FOR SCRAPPING ONLY)

FOR SALE SITE & MAILING
ADDRESS SEE PAGE NO. 25

DPDSSO
PORTSMOUTH, R I

FOR FURTHER INFORMATION SEE INSIDE

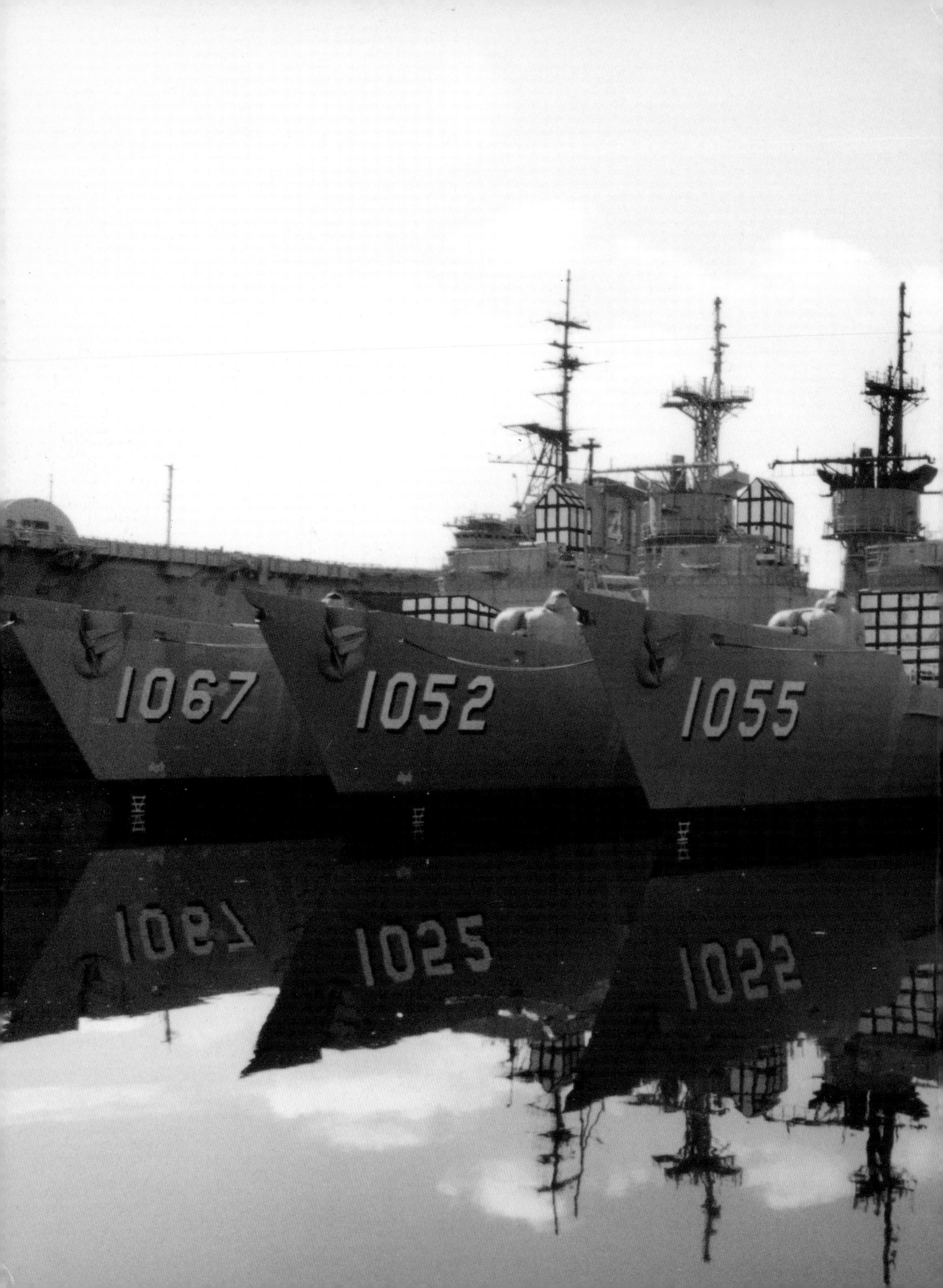
1067
1052
1055

WARSHIP
BONEYARDS

Kit and Carolyn Bonner

MBI Publishing Company

Dedication

Warship Boneyards is dedicated to the thousands of men and women in
the United States Naval Reserve who sacrificed their home lives, careers,
treasures, and youth to heed the call of arms whenever the nation beckoned.
It is also dedicated to the staffs of the Inactive Ship Maintenance Facilities
and the National Defense Reserve Fleets for ensuring that the nation's ships
have been, and will be, ready for the future.

First published in 2001 by MBI Publishing Company,
729 Prospect Avenue, PO Box 1, Osceola, WI
54020-0001 USA

MBI Publishing Company books are also available at
discounts in bulk quantity for industrial or sales-
promotional use. For details write to Special Sales
Manager at Motorbooks International Wholesalers &
Distributors, 729 Prospect Avenue, PO Box 1,
Osceola, WI 54020-0001 USA.

Library of Congress Cataloging-in-Publication Data
Bonner, Kit.
    Warship boneyards / Kit Bonner.
        p. cm.
    Includes index.
    ISBN 0-7603-0870-5 (pbk. : alk. paper)
    1. United States. Navy—Reserve fleets—
History. I. Title.
VA58.4.B68 2001
359.8'3'0973—dc21   00-135002

On the front cover: The wooden-hulled ocean
minesweepers, USS *Enhance* (MSO-437) and USS *Esteem*
(MSO-438), lean against one another in the backwaters of
the Reserve Fleet in Bremerton, Washington, in this July
1997 photos. These 665-ton vessels were commissioned in
1955 and served as replacements for the aging Korean War
era minesweepers. In early 2000, the ships were towed to
the Mare Island Naval Shipyard, and in July 2000, they
were dismantled with giant mechanical claws that ripped
their wooden structures into manageable parts. The
remnants were scooped up and hauled to a recycling plant.
Author's collection

On the frontispiece: This is the title page for a sealed bid
request to purchase the cruisers USS *Los Angeles* (CA-135)
and USS *Galveston* (CLG-3) on April 30, 1975. Both ships
had been stricken at the San Diego inactive ship site and
were up for sale to the highest bidder for scrapping only.
The estimated bid price for the *Los Angeles* was $800,000,
and the *Galveston* was $400,000. *Courtesy L. Cote*

On the title page: The *Iowa*-class battleship USS *New
Jersey* (BB-62) is moored with a nest of *Knox*-class frigates
at the Naval Inactive Ship Maintenance Facility in
Bremerton, Washington, in this July 17, 1998, photograph.
The *New Jersey*, like her three sisters, had been
recommissioned in the early 1980s to form the nucleus of
surface action groups. All were decommissioned after the
end of the Cold War in 1991. The *New Jersey* was placed
out of service on February 28, 1991, and was subsequently
moved to the Philadelphia Naval Shipyard and arrived in
November 1999 (she is now a memorial ship in Camden,
NJ). She and her sisters will be preserved as memorials or
in naval reserve status. The lead ship, the USS *Knox* (FF-
1052), of a 46-ship class of frigates is two ships outboard
from the *New Jersey*. The *Knox* class was commissioned
from 1969 through 1974, and was primarily designed for
escort and antisubmarine work. By 1994 all *Knox*-class
ships had been decommissioned due to cost constraints
and the collapse of the Soviet Union. *Author's collection*

On the back cover: This photo was taken on May 23,
1972, and overlooks the Mare Island reserve facility. In the
foreground are four *Agile*-class wooden-hulled
minesweepers built in the mid-1950s. Just behind them are
10 submarines including the USS *Growler* (SS-577) moored
next to the dock. The *Growler* was designed to carry the
Regulus II guided missile in its oversize bow deck housing.
The diesel/electric boat served from 1958 through 1964 and
was the precursor to the *George Washington*-class ballistic
missile submarine. The *Growler* was stricken in 1980.
Courtesy L. Cote

Edited by Amy Glaser
Designed by LeAnn Kuhlmann

Printed in China

CONTENTS

PREFACE

**"Sweepers, man your brooms.
Sweep down forward and aft.
Don't miss the corners!"**

On many mornings, I was awakened by this unfailing refrain of an aircraft carrier's public address system. I was 14 years old and lived on the hill overlooking the Puget Sound Naval Shipyard in Bremerton, Washington. My father was finishing out his naval career as one of the officers in command of the Bremerton Group of the U.S. Navy's Pacific Reserve Fleet or "warship boneyard." It was 1959, and carriers such as the USS *Coral Sea* (CVA-43) were under repair or being modernized to accommodate heavy jet aircraft. The carriers shared space in the shipyard with two brand-new missile frigates, the USS *King* (DLG-10) and the USS *Coontz* (DLG-9), whose electronic systems and *Terrier* antiaircraft missile batteries represented the future of naval combat. The yard was busy, as were most naval shipyards in the United States, because the Cold War at sea was escalating. The Soviet Navy was entering the international naval community with what would become a world-class navy. The U.S. Navy was about to have its first real threat at sea since the early days of World War II.

Just a stone's throw from the cutting edge of a new generation of American warships were scores of warships of all types quietly resting in the Pacific Reserve Fleet. This was one of the U.S. Navy's many post–World War II warship boneyards. At the conclusion of World War II and the Korean Conflict, hundreds of vessels were put into reserve fleets in coastal areas from the James River in Virginia to Bremerton, Washington. Unlike previous mass decommissionings, these ships were scientifically preserved for potential future use. In theory, they could be quickly recommissioned in 30 days or less for fleet use. The need for these ships was to become commonplace during the years immediately following World War II, although the reactivation process proved longer than 30 days. Battleships such as the USS *New Jersey* (BB-62) and USS *Missouri* (BB-63) reentered fleet service dependent on specific need, and several of the *Essex*-class carriers were recommissioned and modernized for service during the Cold War. However, most of the decommissioned cruisers, destroyers, destroyer escorts, escort carriers, and auxiliaries spent many years quietly awaiting a call to arms that never came. As the years wore on, they were joined by newer ships, and those deemed too old for active service were towed away to the shipbreakers or for use as targets. A very fortunate few were preserved by dedicated organizations that could not bear the thought of a seagoing historical landmark being rendered into vehicles or razor blades.

The only noise ever heard from the ships was an occasional alarm to notify watchmen that one was taking on water or that intruders were in unauthorized locations. Ships such as the famed World War II veterans, battleship USS *Alabama* (BB-60), light cruiser USS *San Diego* (CLAA-53), and the heavily battle-damaged *Essex*-class carrier, USS *Bunker Hill*

The USS *Oriskany* (CV-34) is tied up at Mare Island in 1999. The *Oriskany* had been retired in 1976 and moored in reserve at the inactive ship site in Bremerton, Washington. She was brought down to Mare Island to be dismantled by Pegasus Inc., a shpbreaker. The ship sat due to financial problems, and in late 1999, she was towed to the National Defense Reserve Fleet in Beaumont, Texas. *Author's collection*

(CV-17) just sat gathering seagull droppings and sea growth on their hulls.

A Cornucopia of Artifacts

On nearby piers and in deserted warehouses, other remnants still existed of the great World War II fleet that had defeated the Imperial Japanese Navy just 15 years earlier. Five-inch .38-caliber gun mounts, twin and quad 40mm antiaircraft guns, destroyer whaleboats, and gas masks were stored until they would be needed again. With rare exceptions, the artifacts remained undisturbed, and when it was ultimately certain that the weapons and equipment were obsolete, they were disposed of.

For a young teenager with little to do on the weekend, the Pacific Reserve Fleet was a historical playground without parallel. Wandering around the ships and poking into pierside trash dumpsters, I found a number of treasures that I would not trade for a fortune. I rescued a copy of the USS *Missouri*'s (BB-63) 1945 formal cruise book from the trash bin. It included all of the photographic details of the Japanese surrender in Tokyo Bay. I also liberated a cruise book from the battleship USS *Alabama* (BB-60) that included an autograph of baseball great Bob Feller, who helped his ship win the 1944 Pacific Fleet baseball championship. I even found a Philippine five-peso note especially created by the Imperial Japanese government when it

The U.S. Navy *Virginia-class* nuclear missile cruisers (front to rear) USS *Arkansas* (CGN-41), USS *Mississippi* (CGN-40), and USS *Texas* (CGN-39) steam close together. These ships were spartan looking, but were powerfully armed. The lack of permanent helicopter facilities or *AEGIS* electronic systems capability doomed these ships to an early retirement. *U.S. Navy*

A March 3, 1961, photograph of the USS *Los Angeles* (CA-135) was provided by the Navy to the *San Francisco Call Bulletin* newspaper. The picture was part of this ship's standard press kit for the media. This ship provided concentrated gunfire support to ground forces during the Korean War. *U.S. Navy*

7

This photo was taken on May 23, 1972, and overlooks the Mare Island reserve facility. In the foreground are four *Agile*-class wooden-hulled minesweepers that were built in the mid-1950s. Just behind them are 10 submarines including the USS *Growler* (SS-577), which is moored next to the dock. *Courtesy L. Cote*

successfully invaded and captured the Philippine Islands in 1942. Unfortunately, I did not take any photographs of the shipyard, but my memories of these great ships will never fade. Today, the Puget Sound Naval Shipyard is still active, but on a vastly reduced basis. Few ships are permanently based in Bremerton, and much of the work done by the yard is restricted to breaking up nuclear submarines and surface ships. The once proud dream of the 1980s 600-ship navy, replete with 15 carrier battle groups, surface action groups built around *Iowa*-class battleships, nuclear surface escorts, and scores of nuclear attack and ballistic missile submarines, can be found either in reserve or in a scrap heap.

The battleships USS *Alabama* and USS *Missouri* found homes as museum ships, but the USS *Bunker Hill* and USS *San Diego* were scrapped, as were hundreds of others from reserve fleet anchorages in coastal areas all over the United States. In a life cycle that seems to repeat itself every two generations, the futuristic ships of the early 1960s, such as the missile destroyers *King* and *Coontz*, now sit in the backwaters of the Philadelphia Naval Shipyard awaiting sale to scrap firms. At the dawn of the twenty-first century and another era of cost cutting in the military, these ships now share berths and likely fates with relatively modern *Spruance*-class destroyers and *Oliver Hazard Perry* frigates.

The cruisers USS *Macon* (CA-132) and USS *Wilkes Barre* (CL-103) are moored in what was once known as cruisers row at the Philadelphia Naval Shipyard. *U.S. Navy Cruiser Sailors Association*

Nearly 40 years after leaving the Puget Sound Naval Shipyard, I returned to represent California's Governor Pete Wilson at the inactivation ceremony of the world's last nuclear cruiser, the USS *California* (CGN-36) in August 1998. It was a bittersweet reunion, as I knew this beautiful and powerful ship would soon be re-duced to a hulk and join others awaiting the inevitable scrap pile. The *California*, like her sister the USS *South Carolina* (CGN-37) and her half sisters of the *Virginia* class, had been deemed too expensive to maintain and operate. Many of the nuclear surface ships and attack and ballistic missile submarines had bypassed the customary warship life cycle and were being dismantled without spending a period in the inactive fleet. This was also true of other vessels such as the four-ship *Kidd*-class destroyers whose paint barely oxidized before being disposed of.

The inactive fleet at Bremerton was still there, only the ships were different. The carriers USS *Independence* (CV-62) and USS *Midway* (CV-41) were moored where the *Essex*-class carrier USS *Hornet* (CV-12) and missile cruisers USS *Chicago* (CG-11) and USS *Oklahoma City* (CG-5) were once preserved. The true difference at Bremerton between 1959 and 1998 was the number of ships in the warship boneyard. With the development of sophisticated electronic warfare systems and the increased war-fighting capability in each new ship to join the U.S. arsenal, the day of building huge numbers of warships is all but over. A single *Arleigh Burke*-class destroyer has more destructive power than an entire squad-ron of *Fletcher*-class destroyers. As a consequence, the need for large numbers of reserve fleet bastions has passed into history.

I am grateful to have witnessed the sheer power of the United States Navy at its apex at the end of World War II, and thankfully I was able to wander among historic ships as they rested in reserve status.

Five ex-Soviet navy submarines are beached in the backwater of a Russian port. From left to right are a *Foxtrot* patrol diesel submarine, two *Echo I* nuclear attack boats, an *Echo II* nuclear cruise missile submarine, and a *Yankee I* nuclear ballistic missile boat. *Greenpeace*

Warship Boneyards tells the story of the United States Navy at rest and the ultimate disposal of its ships when they are no longer needed for the active defense of the nation. It tracks the development of improved methods of preserving the nation's most expensive military assets and how this has benefited national defense over the last 75 years. *Warship Boneyards* also puts a face on the historical aspect of the ships that made such distinguished contributions in the defense of freedom.
—*Kit Bonner*

ACKNOWLEDGMENTS

Special thanks to the following for their assistance and guidance in the preparation of *Warship Boneyards*. Without their help, this book could not have been written.

Larry Cote, naval historian and maritime photographer
Joe Flaherty and staff, Inactive Ship Maintenance Facility–Philadelphia Navy Yard
Joe Peccocaro, Suisun Bay Reserve Fleet

Jeff Lee, Southwest Marine Corporation
Pete Galassi and Bob Callaghan, Inactive Ship Maintenance Facility–Bremerton, Washington
Rick Burgess, Navy League
John Baker, USS *Oklahoma City* Association
George Bisharat, Vallejo Naval and Historical Museum
Dawn Stitzel, U.S. Naval Institute
Jim Kern, Vallejo Naval and Historical Museum

Probably one of the most well known of all warship boneyards is the U.S. Navy's Inactive Ship Maintenance Facility at the Philadelphia Naval Shipyard. From the earliest days of the steel navy, it has been the customary site where ships of the Atlantic Fleet are stored. In this July 30, 1974, photograph, the surplus cruisers USS Topeka (CLG-8), USS Boston (CAG-1), USS Des Moines (CA-134), USS Salem (CA-139), and command ship USS Northampton (CC-1) sit facing Broad Street at Wharf L. With the exception of the Salem, now a museum ship, and the Des Moines, all others have been scrapped. The Des Moines, known as the "eyesore," was still moored there as of the turn of the century. U.S.N.I.

Chapter One
THE WARSHIP BONEYARD

ORIGINS AND OVERVIEW

Nations build warships to defeat a specific adversary, protect national interests, or enhance national growth through the introduction of the nations' policies beyond their borders. Commerce and industry are also the driving forces behind the creation and sustenance of navies ("trade follows the flag"), and naval forces have often paved the way for new trade, willing markets, and resources. When the threat disappears, policies have been successful, and/or business is satisfied, navies often fall into disuse. In fact, ships are the most expensive and visible of all government equipment, and are generally the first targets for budget cuts. Few nations have been able to sustain large numbers of ships in active status for an extended period of time without very compelling and popularly supported reasons. Classic incentives include long-term wars at sea or persistent threats to national security and commerce by other nations or pirates. The United States Navy has been the acknowledged superpower at sea in the latter half of the twentieth century due to its growth during World War II and the Cold War. However, its reign was not in the same league as Great Britain's Royal Navy during its prime.

This photo was taken on November 1999 at Wharf L, Inactive Ship Maintenance Facility, Philadelphia Naval Shipyard. Twenty-five years later, the cruisers *Topeka, Boston, Des Moines, Northampton,* and *Salem* are replaced by the fleet auxiliaries USS *Sylvania* (AFS-2), USS *Milwaukee* (AOR-2), USS *Savannah* (AOR-4), and USS *Kalamazoo* (AOR-6). The 1990s reduction in active U.S. Navy combat ships caused the inactivity of their support force. *Author's collection*

It was necessary for Great Britain to protect the trade routes and Colonies during much of the seventeenth, eighteenth, and nineteenth centuries, thus the Royal Navy became an established institution at sea. It was said that "the sun never set on the British Empire," and its navy paved the way and protected the routes. That day has now passed into history, yet the memory of the worldwide reach of the Royal Navy has not disappeared. A more recent period of battleless conflict that required large numbers of active warships was the 1945 to 1991 Cold War between the Western allies and the Soviet bloc. In the end, international quarrels and issues were resolved, and the combat ships became inactive.

Ships that are outdated or no longer needed for active service often spend time in a warship boneyard awaiting their fate. These out-of-the-way sites have been numerous at times and heavily crowded, especially after World War II. Warship boneyards, inactive fleet sites, reserve ship depots, or deserted ship anchorages have been in existence since navies first plied the seas.

The boneyards at the beginning of the twenty-first century are no different. There are a growing number of sites worldwide where combat ships from World War II and subsequent conflicts await their disposition. The most prominent have been the surface ships, including aircraft carriers and battleships that are identified by the slowly oxidizing gray paint and lack of exterior equipment, which has been stuck below deck or stored ashore. To the facilities for the more traditional inactive surface ship facilities have been added space for the rapidly growing fleet of nuclear submarines that require special processing. In the United States, the Puget Sound Naval Shipyard in Bremerton, Washington, employs a comprehensive nuclear recycling system that safely removes and transports nuclear materials to preplanned areas for permanent disposal. More than 100 nuclear attack and ballistic missile submarines that were built for the Cold War are currently being processed, and the ex–Soviet navy has a similar number requiring the same treatment. There is little funding for a comparable job to that performed by the U.S. Navy, and international watchdog agencies are attempting to ensure that no nuclear accidents occur due to careless handling of nuclear components. Due to the highly toxic nature of nuclear components, it is probable that the United States and former Soviet Union will enter into a partnership agreement to dispose of their decommissioned nuclear boats.

In the past, warship boneyards have often been regarded as nuisances to city planners and waterfront residents who complain about the view they offer. The possibility of a nuclear accident adds an entirely new dimension to the definition of warship boneyard. It becomes something to be feared.

Warship boneyards can also be created involuntarily through accident, battle damage, or scuttling. On September 8, 1923, just after 9 P.M., seven modern 1,149-ton flush deck, four-piper destroyers of the U.S. Navy's Destroyer Squadron Eleven piled up on the rocks at Point Honda, California. The "Devil's Jaw," as this area of the central California coastline is known, has claimed 26 ships, including the 7 destroyers that were steaming into the fog at 20 knots. The ships followed one another onto the beach or the rocks. On the morning of September 9th, the daylight revealed that the USS *Delphy* (DD-261), USS *Young* (DD-312), USS *S P Lee* (DD-310), USS *Woodbury* (DD-309), USS *Nicholas* (DD-311), USS *Chauncey* (DD-296), and USS *Fuller* (DD-297) were helplessly impaled on the jagged rocks of the Devil's Jaw. They had been added to the already-existing commercial vessel graveyard.

The USS *Kennedy* (DD-306) and USS *Farragut* (DD-304) struck bottom, yet were eventually successful in extricating themselves. This accident was the worst in U.S. Naval history at the time, and 23 men lost their lives. Attempts to salvage the ships were made, but the situation was hopeless. The remains were sold for $1,035 to a salvager in 1925.

There were few images of Great Britain's Royal Navy in the early 1800s that speak so much to the period as Turner's *The Fighting Temeraire*. British artist Joseph Mallord William Turner painted this work in 1838, and it is now on display in the National Gallery in London. It depicts the end of an era as a tired wooden sail-powered warship is towed by a steam tug to her final berth. The advent of metal hulls and steam power spelled doom for a type of warship that was centuries old. *Treasure Island Museum*

The Pacific Reserve Fleet at San Diego, California, in July 1969. The crowded docks play host to a who's who of World War II and later warships including the Korean War veteran USS *Philippine Sea* (CV-47) (lower left corner), and the USS *San Jacinto* (CVL-30/AVT-5) (left center) from whose decks a 20-year-old naval aviator, former President George Bush, flew a torpedo bomber (TBM) during World War II in the Pacific. Moored next to the light carrier are the light cruisers USS *Amsterdam* (CL-101*)* and USS *Astoria* (CL-90). Both cruisers escorted the fast carriers during their raids on the Japanese home islands in 1945. All were scrapped within three years after this photograph. *Courtesy L. Cote*

The *Iowa*-class battleship USS *New Jersey* (BB-62) is pictured at her new berth at Pier 4 in the Philadelphia Naval Shipyard. She arrived on November 11, 1999, from her former home in Bremerton, Washington, and was moored opposite the *Forrestal*-class aircraft carrier USS *America* (CV-66). The *America* was stricken from the Navy list on August 9, 1996, and is destined for the shipbreakers. The *New Jersey* became a museum ship. *Author's collection*

Warship boneyards are also created by scuttling and battle damage such as the wholesale destruction of the German High Seas Fleet at Scapa Flow in the Orkneys in 1919. The resurrected American fleet in Pearl Harbor (1941–1942) and the expatriate Dutch Fleet in the Netherlands East Indies (1942) became short-lived warship boneyards. War was a breeding ground for boneyards.

Naval warfare continued unabated in the South Pacific throughout 1942 to 1944. There are many small—and a few massive—warship boneyards to remind us of the devastation of war. Dozens of dead ships litter much of Truk Lagoon in the Pacific, and Allied and Japanese warships are scattered in Ironbottom Sound in the Solomon Islands. Night after night Allied warships that could still steam and fire their weapons met well-armed, high-speed Japanese naval forces that were intent on providing

support to the Imperial Japanese Army in the Solomons. Ironbottom Sound became a killing ground for the pride of both navies. It was named after a hemorrhage of naval might that left the Japanese defeated and the Allies bloodied.

From a voluntary standpoint, most seafaring nations have often found it necessary to inactivate its warships at one time or another. In the seventeenth, eighteenth, and nineteenth centuries, Great Britain, Holland, and France periodically immobilized their combat ships. Reasons for ship inactivation ranged from the cessation of war to accelerated obsolescence due to advances in technology. Navies that routinely operated up to 400 ships were pared down to fewer than 200 ships during peacetime. The introduction of steam propulsion in the early 1800s progressively rendered entire fleets of sail-powered ships out of date. Technical advances were also responsible for ships going to an early grave. Many European navies that adjusted to steam and the paddle wheel had to make another adaptation by the middle of the nineteenth century when screw propulsion was proved superior. Paddle wheel-propelled warships followed older sail-powered vessels into premature obsolescence.

Navies retired their ships to fresh water or tidal basins and often sheathed the hulls in copper to protect

The Chilean Navy *Crucero O'Higgins*, the former USS *Brooklyn* (CL-40), is shown at the Chilean Navy Station at Talcahauno in October 1992. From there she was towed to India for scrapping. The old cruiser had served in two navies for 56 years. Chile, which had been her home for 41 years, employed the ship on near continuous active service, and she was passed directly to the scrapyard with little time in between. The *Brooklyn/O'Higgins* was the last active all-gun cruiser, and with her passing, an era came to an end. *Author's collection*

One of the first of a new breed of American warships, the USS *Chicago* (CL-14) joined sisters USS *Atlanta* and USS *Boston* (ABC cruisers) and paved the way for the new navy of the 1880s. The *Chicago* was renamed the USS *Alton* (IX-5) and ended up in a warship boneyard at Pearl Harbor. She sank while being towed to San Francisco in July 1936. *Treasure Island Museum*

and spent his final years without a ship to command. The "Father of the American Navy" died penniless of pneumonia in Paris, France, 10 years later. He died on the eve of his receiving his first commission in the new United States Navy.

There was little done to preserve the ships during the late 1700s to early 1880s except to guard against looters and thieves, and to store much of the ships' equipment and stores (rope, sail, and weapons) ashore in protected warehouses.

against destructive sea organisms, including wood worms. These ships were laid up "in ordinary," which was close to be being placed in reserve, or put in "mothballs" in modern-day parlance. Paltry maintenance costs were derived from the government's "ordinary" naval budget as opposed to commissioned service that would warrant a full roster of officers, crew, munitions, sails, and victuals. Ships laid up "in ordinary" looked much like barren hulls with sticks standing up where yards and sails had once been.

Ships are not the only part of navies left ignored in the backwaters. The officers and men were also laid up, which made most ordinary seamen or landsmen who rejoined their families very happy. The crew members were discharged pending some future need, and ports and naval bases were crowded with officers, on half or no pay, seeking an appointment on any naval or commercial ship. In a sense, the officers were also part of the warship boneyard. One of the most famous officers cast ashore with no prospects for future employment in the Continental/U.S. Navy was John Paul Jones. His stunning victory over the modern British frigate HMS *Serapis* from the deck of the elderly *Bon Homme Richard* on September 23, 1779, was truly one of the greatest naval actions of any war. In June 1781, Jones was rewarded with the captaincy of the brand-new 74-gun *America*, the most powerful ship of the line built for the new nation. Before Jones could go to sea, however, the unfinished vessel was presented to France for her valued contribution to the Revolutionary cause. Jones briefly served Catherine the Great in Russia,

This photograph was taken just days before the USS *Alton* (IX-5), ex–USS *Chicago* (CL-14), sank while being towed to the West Coast from Pearl Harbor. After a successful career as a cruiser, the first steel combatant in the U.S. Navy was used as a submarine tender at Pearl Harbor from December 1919 until September 1923. Like so many older ships, her roles became less important with age and after decommissioning on September 30, 1923, she became a barracks ship. In essence, she had become part of a backwaters warship boneyard. She was renamed *Alton* in 1928 to allow her name to be used for the new treaty cruiser USS *Chicago* (CA-29). *Author's collection*

The USS *Kennedy* (DD-306) at high speed in the mid-1920s. She and six other destroyers miraculously survived the night of September 8, 1923, when seven sister ships ran aground at Point Honda, north of Santa Barbara, California. The *Kennedy* was stricken from the Navy in November 1930, and was replaced by a destroyer that had been quietly sitting in reserve for years in the "red lead row" at the San Diego Navy Base. *Author's collection*

Tar and pitch were used as preservatives, but there weren't many known scientific methods to be applied. A small number of officers and crew were assigned to protect the ships, repair leaks, and ensure that the ships did not slip their moorings. Ships were monitored to determine if there were any serious leaks. Frigates, sloops, and great ships of the line were observed to determine if they were lower in the water from day to day. Contemporary warships are also monitored in the same fashion, but with the added protection of an alarm system to notify inactive ship maintenance facility managers of any leakage. Today, telescopes and binoculars can easily be found near the inactive ship facility for modern managers to watch their charges just like the predecessors of centuries ago. There is little difference between a ship laid up "in ordinary" during the nineteenth century, and the *Iowa*-class battleship, USS *New Jersey* (BB-62), sitting in mothballs at the Philadelphia Naval Shipyard in the early twenty-first century (now a memorial ship in Camden, NJ). Both ships have that forlorn and somber look that can only be rectified by a fresh coat of paint and the living force of officers and men swarming their decks.

Many boneyards have been in use for centuries, especially in Great Britain, where ships were laid up or beached in the backwaters of popular naval bases. Royal Navy vessels selected for disposal have been sent to Inverness or Inverkeithing, whereas in France, older defanged combat ships are often tethered to one another at Brest or Cherbourg. Italian warships no longer in use can often be seen at La Spezia.

Generally, most of the world's smaller navies do not maintain inactive fleet sites or reserve fleet facilities. The ships are in use until they are only good for scrap. South American navies are prime examples of this policy. Several are still utilizing ex–U.S. Navy destroyers and auxiliaries that were built during World War II. The Chilean Navy employed the light cruiser ex–USS *Brooklyn* (CL-40) as its flagship, *Crucero O'Higgins*, from its purchase date from the U.S. Navy in 1951 until it was decommissioned on January 14, 1992. The *Brooklyn* was originally commissioned on September 30, 1937, and served for a combined total of 55 years in both navies. The Mexican Navy still carries the former USS *John Rodgers* (DD-574) (*Cuitlahauc*), a museum-quality *Fletcher*-class destroyer, as an active fleet unit. The *Rodgers*, in remarkably good condition and configured in World War II weaponry, was commissioned on February 9, 1943, for the U.S. Navy and was later transferred to the Mexican Navy in August 1970. Like so many other recipients of

Eagle Boat number PE-12 was at the San Diego Navy Base on July 19, 1924, after it was lost at sea for four days. Her steam turbine propulsion became disabled and a concentrated search failed to locate the wayward World War I Henry Ford production line antisubmarine vessel. Most of the 60 *Eagle Boats* found their way into various reserve fleets, including the 10 that were tied up at the Mare Island Naval Shipyard. *Treasure Island Museum*

U.S. Navy combat ships, the Mexican Navy has derived more service (in this case, 30 years) than the original owners.

The United States Navy and Its Warship Boneyards

The United States Navy was a relative newcomer to the international naval community, and at the end of the Revolutionary War, the Navy sold off its last ship (the *Alliance*) in 1785. The United States government planned to rely on the goodwill of its people and nonaggressive intentions to exclude it from harm at sea. The new nation also naively hoped for protection by its former enemy, Great Britain, as both nations had many business relationships in common. It was further rationalized that if a need arose, a navy could quickly be built or commandeered for use in commerce raiding or coast defense. The wars with the Barbary Pirates and the War of 1812 graphically drove home the folly of this thinking, and the United States Navy was born. It was small in number at first, but grew with westward expansion to ultimately gain and defend its protectorates in the Pacific.

Until the American Civil War from 1861 to 1865, the U.S. Navy had a small number of warships compared to other seagoing nations. Its steam frigates were the envy of the world's navies, but were few in number. Typically, the United States operated in far-flung areas around the world and showed the

On November 21, 1947, three *Bagley*-class 1,500-ton ex–U.S. Navy destroyers are being towed from Pearl Harbor to the West Coast for scrapping. From left to right are the USS *Craven* (DD-382*)*, USS *Bagley* (DD-386), and USS *Helm* (DD-388). Hundreds of older vessels were sold or scrapped within months after World War II and spent little time in the many warship boneyards that were created to hold surplus warships. *Author's collection* flag, and little thought was given to combined fleet operations. Most of the older vessels were laid up "in ordinary" at various locations or converted for other tasks such as receiving ships or temporary barracks for crews. Ships would come out of reserve for a specific purpose, and in some instances, be decommissioned again until needed. When the ships were too old for any use, they were broken up. The process of decommissioning and breaking ships changed with the secession of several southern states from the Union in 1861 and the resultant civil war. The Union initiated a massive building program that included the development and construction of naval warfare's most revolutionary combat ships—the ironclads and monitors. The Union Navy learned as it went along, and by the end of the war, the South was in ruins and the United States Navy, comprising over 500 vessels of all types, was one of the most powerful navies in the world.

In the years following the Civil War, the armed forces of the nation were slowly allowed to deteriorate and assume a back seat to all other government operations. This scenario was repeated many times in American naval history. There was no active enemy expected to challenge the United States in the foreseeable future, and much of that future lay westward—with it would come expansion and progress. Isolationism was a byword, and the thousands of miles of ocean between other major powers and the continental United States provided a natural barrier.

In the wake of the spectacular victory over the Confederacy, the Navy was all but disbanded. It was treated similarly during the post-Revolutionary and War of 1812 days, and had difficulty prying funds from the U.S. Congress to maintain any semblance of a fleet at sea. Even money to pay for coal to fire the engines was difficult to secure.

War-built and -outfitted frigates, ironclads, and monitors were allowed to rust and age beyond usefulness in the backwaters adjacent to naval shipyards, which themselves were stretched trying to secure limited operating funds. Ultimately, most of these vessels lost their potential as weapons. Sophisticated means of preservation had not come into vogue as yet. Had the techniques even been available, by the time these ships were reactivated they were obsolete and of no use in the wars to come. Similar to the triumph of steam over sail power, what had been a great navy in 1865 was rendered into one of limited capability by technological innovations and advances in naval design during the latter half of the nineteenth century. Great Britain, France, and Germany had carefully observed the naval war between the States and were updating their navies with lessons learned. These were not navies primarily driven by economics and the need to fund territorial expansion to the West, as was that of the United States. Rather, these navies were supported by decades of inborn national pride, and the need to protect seaborne commerce and colonies abroad. Much of the wealth and stability of the more prominent European nations was dependent on trade and affordable foreign resources.

Within 15 years of the conclusion of the Civil War, the United States Navy had fallen to a 12th-rate

This is the colorful headquarters office barge of the Maritime Administration's Suisun Bay Reserve Fleet in northern California. The ex-barrack ship often has bunting flying while it is on public display at various times of the year. There are high-powered telescopes around the boneyard (directly forward and in one of the former 20mm antiaircraft gun tubes in this photo) to look at the dozens of ships moored in the channel. Work boats and tugs that transport personnel out to the fleet to perform maintenance are tethered alongside. *Author's collection*

Not all warship boneyards contain just ships. The lower hold of the Suisun Bay station ship has a feast of former ships' bells, engine room telegraphs, binnacles, and the like. On occasion, a museum or college asks for a bell and other equipment to be donated or loaned. Several colleges and universities have bells from *Victory* ships that were named after the school. *Author's collection*

In a rather rare photograph, the battleship *Iowa* leads her three sisters in this 1954 photo. These are certainly the most magnificent warships ever built and symbolize the height of the twentieth century's U.S. naval arsenal. All four ships fought in wars after World War II, but the biggest fight for them was to be preserved. By 2000 it was decided to retain them as memorials or inactive reserve. As long as there are supporters and admirers of the U.S. Navy, these ships will survive. *U.S. Navy*

fighting force behind Turkey and China. Finally, its leaders and the U.S. Congress began to understand the value of being a power at sea, as well as on land, and initiated a buildup of its naval forces in the 1880s. The first steel warship with rifled barrels was completed in 1884. The USS *Chicago* was a 4,500-ton protected cruiser and a good start toward a new navy. The process was slow and ponderous at first. By the time the Spanish-American War began in 1898, the U.S. Navy was sufficiently capable to engineer the defeat of a major European power, albeit one that had seen better days. In 1900, two years after the war started, the Navy consisted of 84 active warships and a similar number in repair or under construction. In addition, there were 76 vessels out of commission that sat in reserve sites located in various ports in the United States or U.S. protectorates such as Mare Island, California; Norfolk, Virginia; and Cavite, Manila Bay. Most of these vessels were far out of date and of no practical value to the Navy.

It was not until the end of World War I in 1918 that the United States Navy had a huge excess of modern warships. The submarine menace posed by Germany was so great that the construction priority in U.S. shipyards was for antisubmarine- or destroyer-type ships. Although the United States was only formally committed for the last two years of World War I (1917 and 1918), hundreds of escort and anti-submarine ships were built for the cause. Most of

these ships were immediately laid up and never saw any form of combat.

There were 267 flush deck, four-piper World War I destroyers commissioned, and only 39 were commissioned before the armistice was signed. Shipyards also built 440 submarine chasers (SC), and 100 were transferred to the French Navy. There were also 60 experimental *Eagle Boat* patrol craft (PE), and a large number of cargo and troop transports and auxiliaries of all types. By the early 1920s, the United States Navy was a world-class navy, but without sufficient funding to maintain its newly acquired ships at sea. Past practice was that at the end of a conflict, the U.S. Navy would sustain a bare minimum of ships on active status and either sell unneeded ships to another country or allow the inactive ships to rot in the backwaters of a tidal basin near a naval facility. The magnitude of the post–World War I fleet called for a different approach, and the phenomenon of ship storage or assemblage on a massive scale was inaugurated. The nation's taxpayers had contributed too much to the building of a modern navy to have it immediately broken up. Another consideration was the fact that the world was still unstable, and a powerful navy was important to national defense. This was not restricted to the U.S. Navy. The navies of France, Italy, and Great Britain were also faced with severe cost cutting, and had to cut back the number of maintained active sea units. Harbors in Portsmouth, England; Brest, France; and Taranto, Italy, became repositories of World War I veterans just like San Diego, California; and Philadelphia, Pennsylvania.

During World War II, the U.S. Navy saw action in every theater of operations. A prewar naval buildup began during the mid-1930s that included withdrawing ships held in reserve. The effort was dramatically heightened in 1940 when the probability of Great Britain's defeat by Nazi Germany loomed. Ship construction accelerated when the United States entered the war in December 1941 and did not subside until the end of the war. As in the previous World War, several ships were completed long after the combat formally came to an end. At the end of World War II in 1945, the United States Navy had 1,308 combat ships in commission, including 40 fleet carriers, 79 escort carriers, 24

The USS *Hornet* (CV-12) at her permanent mooring in the now-closed Alameda Naval Air Station on San Francisco Bay in August 1999. The *Hornet* had been part of the inactive fleet in Bremerton for years and was rescued from the shipbreakers. A dedicated group of aircraft carrier enthusiasts and supporters worked tirelessly to preserve the old ship. She also sports equipment cannibalized from the ex–USS *Oriskany* (CV-34), a longtime resident carrier at the Mare Island Naval Shipyard. *Author's collection*

battleships, 93 cruisers, 263 submarines, and 809 destroyers. The number of vessels was doubled by the time World War II ended. There wasn't a need to maintain a huge force at sea. There were some immediate postwar congressional proposals that called for a navy of 1,079 combat vessels with 800 placed in reserve status. This did not include the hundreds of auxiliaries, patrol craft, and minesweepers that were destined for inactivity. All but 127 major combat vessels found their way into mothballs or to the shipbreakers by 1950. More than 2,000 ships were preserved in locations all around the United States, and periodically some were withdrawn for war service or for other purposes. The Korean War from 1950 to 1953 witnessed the rebirth of nearly all of the *Essex*-class carriers, 3 battleships, 5 cruisers, and 170 destroyer-type vessels, as well as innumerable support craft. An immense number of ships remained in mothballs, however, until it was determined they were too outdated to be of any real value. In the early 1960s and 1970s, identifiable groups and classes of ships were disposed of by one means or another.

Generally age, condition, and the price of scrap metal were the major factors considered.

After the conclusion of World War II, the Korean Conflict and Vietnam War were directly intertwined with a new dimension in naval warfare—the Cold War between the Soviet Union and the Western allies. This resulted in a further release of ships from their respective reserve sites, but the need declined as the years went by. Warship building programs in the 1960s, 1970s, and 1980s that emphasized modern electronics and weaponry as well as nuclear power systematically eliminated the necessity for any significant number of older and obsolete ships to be reactivated. Economics and no visible enemy to fight caused the early retirement of many ships. In the life cycle of combat ships, those once considered futuristic during the Cold War now rest quietly in various inactive ship facilities. In the dawn of the twenty-first century, those ships have become obsolete and many occupied warship boneyards previously occupied by ships left over from past wars. The Gulf War in 1991 witnessed the last significant use of many U.S. warships.

The Inactive Ship Maintenance Facility at the Philadelphia Naval Shipyard in mid-November 1999. This facility has been open for business for over 100 years and has accommodated surplus destroyers after World War I including the *Wickes/Clemson* four piper, flush deck, World War II *Fletcher*-class destroyers, and *Spruance* and *Kidd* classes. At the bottom center is the *Oliver Hazard Perry*-class USS *Stark* (FFG-31), which on May 17, 1987, gained international attention when she was struck by two *Exocet* missiles fired by an Iraqi French-made *Mirage F-1* attack aircraft. The *Stark* was nearly sunk and 37 members of her crew lost their lives. *Author's collection*

When the war ended, many more ships were decommissioned and joined their Cold War sisters in one inactive ship site or another. Today, ships of the United States Navy and other formerly powerful navies have again fallen into a period of decline, and many await an almost predetermined fate.

Notorious Warship Boneyards

The definition of a warship boneyard must also include boneyards that were involuntarily created.

An early example occurred in 1588, when 130 of the Spanish armada's ships attempted to defeat England's smaller navy. After a series of severe storms destroyed them, the Spanish ships were strewn all over the Irish coastline. The twentieth century, however, has played host to the most infamous of involuntarily created warship boneyards.

During the 1904–1905 Russo-Japanese War, a modern Japanese Navy systematically bottled up Russian naval units at Port Arthur in Manchuria as

An Indian worker at the 30-mile-long shipbreakers' beach at Alang, India, throws dunnage onto a makeshift fire from a ship that is being cut up for scrap. A commercial freighter lies on the beach in the background. Ships including those that are ex-Soviet and U.S. Navy are beached at monthly extreme high tides and workers then swarm over the ships and cut them up with hacksaws, acetylene torches, and anything else they can find. At least 100 men, women, and children perish per week in primitive slavelike conditions. They earn less than $350 U.S. per year. The dead are generally burned in a collective fire on the beach. This scandal has caused an international uproar and investigation into ship-scrapping practices with the temporary side effect of ships overcrowding naval reserve sites around the world. *Greenpeace*

This photo was taken on November 27, 1942, in Toulon Harbor, France. In the center of the photograph, the modern battleship *Strasbourg* settles to the bottom after being scuttled by her crew. Just beyond her is the cruiser *Colbert,* engulfed in flames. This involuntarily created warship boneyard netted 72 warships, although several were later raised and repaired. The *Strasbourg* was raised by the Italian Navy in July 1943, but was sunk again by Allied bombers in August 1944. The French raised her and she served in that navy until 1955. *Treasure Island Museum*

part of its support of army operations. The Japanese wanted to eject the Russians from the area and remain in it themselves. The public focus of the war quickly evolved from a ground campaign to active naval warfare. In a series of skirmishes that concluded soon after the famous Battle of the Tsushima on May 27 and 28, 1905, Port Arthur became a boneyard of more than 30 sunken or damaged Russian vessels. Japanese shore batteries of heavy artillery played a part in creating the boneyard. After a bloody series of

battles, the Imperial Japanese Army was able to gain a position that overlooked the harbor. In December 1904, a devastating barrage of gunfire caused substantial damage to ships at anchor, and the Russians decided that five battleships and two cruisers should be scuttled join the others resting on the shallow bottom of Port Arthur. Another battleship and numerous destroyers and other craft were later damaged, and the demolition of the Russian squadron was complete. To compensate for losses incurred during the naval war, the Japanese raised, repaired, and incorporated four Russian battleships and two cruisers into their fleet.

The second involuntary boneyard was the result of the collapse of the Triple Alliance, and shortly thereafter Germany agreed to an armistice beginning on November 11, 1918, ending World War I. During World War I, the German High Seas Fleet, which posed the first serious threat to Great Britain's Royal Navy in nearly 100 years, was forced into an ignominious surrender 10 days after the Armistice. The defeated navy had to suffer humiliation on a scale

The U.S. Navy's fast carriers steamed close to the Japanese home islands in July 1945 to look for anything of value to destroy. Primary targets were warships of the Imperial Japanese Navy and aircraft that might oppose an Allied landing on Japan itself. In a number of out-of-the-way coves and inlets, Allied aircraft found suitable naval targets, but in Kure Bay, they found a number of big prizes. The IJN *Amagi*, a 20,450-ton carrier completed 11 months earlier, was sunk on July 24, 1945, and here she lies on her starboard side in this spectacular image. The carrier had no combat career except being bombed and sunk as part of the Imperial Japanese boneyard fleet in Kure Bay. *U.S.A.F.*

The USS *Chandler* (DD-994) is pictured here in August 1998 as she sits in the Pacific Reserve Fleet in Bremerton, Washington. This *Kidd*-class destroyer, earlier promised to the Shah of Iran before he was ousted from power, became American property on July 6, 1981. She was active in the "tanker wars" of the 1980s, and illegal drug suppression in the eastern Pacific in the late 1990s. She and the other three *Kidd*-class destroyers will have an undetermined future. *Author's collection*

unknown to any professional navy and had to sail 70 major fleet units through a 6-mile-wide channel 8 miles in length artificially created by 370 warships of the Allied Grand Fleet. The Germans had hoped for a foggy day in the Firth of Forth to conceal their shame, but a misty sun exposed the trail of defeated ships led by the British cruiser HMS *Cardiff*. It wasn't known until after the war that these same ships had been part of a plan to make one last valiant sortie against the Allied navies on October 29th. The plan might have worked had it not been for a mutiny by German enlisted crews. They were sick of the war and its deprivations, and they sensed certain death with this new scheme.

After the shameful sail-by, the German fleet, with guns disabled and no ammunition, was relocated to Scapa Flow, in the Orkney Islands. The fleet

consisted of 84 vessels, including 10 battleships, 6 battlecruisers, 8 light cruisers, and 50 destroyer-types. At Scapa Flow the ships swung at anchor and were manned by skeleton crews. The debates over the terms of the Armistice, and ultimately what penalties Germany would suffer, dragged out through the spring and summer of 1919. The High Seas Fleet was to have been interred by the Allies, but a growing concern over their fate caused the German commander Admiral von Reuter to order a mass scuttling. On June 21, 1919, ships began to settle to the bottom of one of the Royal Navy's primary anchorages. British units assigned to monitor the captured fleet were temporarily detached elsewhere and there was little that could be done to prevent the sinkings. All but a handful of destroyers and a battleship were saved by the British crews. Never in the history of naval warfare had so powerful a fleet been lost without a shot being fired. The warship boneyard created by dispirited German crews at Scapa Flow was the last act of defiance of a defeated navy.

The High Seas Fleet sinking at Scapa Flow was, however, nearly equaled 23 years later with the scuttling and destruction of the French Fleet at its naval base at Toulon. France had been defeated by Nazi Germany and was forced to agree to an armistice that emasculated the French government and immobilized the armed forces, including a strong naval establishment. On June 22, 1940, the agreement was signed and went into effect. It included the creation of a vassal state in the south of France that was governed from Vichy. The French Fleet was cast in a peculiar position not to become an adjunct to the German Navy, and at the same time it was not allowed to flee to the Allies and fight for their cause. Within days of the French surrender, units of the French Fleet moored in British ports were captured with little bloodshed. To prevent the possibility of French naval forces in North Africa from becoming belligerent, the Royal Navy attacked the French units at Mersel-Kebir near Oran on July 3, 1940. Most of the French vessels, including the modern battleship *Strasbourg*, escaped to Toulon.

For the next 29 months, there was little activity with the French Fleet at its naval bases in North Africa or Toulon. On November 8, 1942, Operation Torch began with the Allied invasion of French North Africa and quickly prompted local French naval units to come out and fight. They were met by Allied warships including the light cruiser USS *Brooklyn* (CL-40), and most of the French ships were either sunk or heavily damaged. The landings in North Africa caused alarm in Berlin, and the terms of the Franco-German Armistice were violated when Hitler occupied Toulon. The bulk of the remaining French Fleet was in Toulon and was either moored or undergoing war damage repairs. On November 27, 1940, an elite German Panzer Corps occupied Toulon, but not in time to prevent dedicated French sailors from scuttling or burning 16 submarines and 3 battleships, including the *Strasbourg*, *Dunkerque*, and *Provence*. They also destroyed 7 cruisers, including the *Colbert* and *Foch*, as well as 46 destroyers, torpedo boats, and various fleet train auxiliaries. The total loss was a staggering 72 valuable warships, transforming the Toulon Naval Base into a warship boneyard. This was a shameful loss of fine combat ships, but it was better for the Allied cause than to allow these ships to be seized by the Germans.

The war in the Pacific against the Imperial Japanese Navy from 1941 to 1945 resulted in the

The hulks of the nuclear surface navy haunt the Puget Sound Naval Shipyard in August 1998. From right to left are the former USS *Long Beach* (CGN-9), USS *Mississippi* (CGN-40), USS *Virginia* (CGN-38),and USS *Texas* (CGN-39). The process to inactivate a nuclear surface ship is costly and highly regulated for safety reasons. Old sailors nearly weep at the sight of these once proud ships that wait for a scrapper to tow them away. *Author's collection*

This is what the public comes to see at Suisun Bay, where up to 500 ships have been stored. In this 1988 aerial photograph, the anchorage has fewer ships than the glory days of the late 1940s. Ships come and go like clockwork, and orchestrating their arrival and departure is a complex task for the fleet managers. The station ship (APL) can be seen to the center right near the shoreline. *Courtesy Joe Peccoraro, Suisun Bay Reserve Fleet*

destruction of more than 300 front line combat units. By mid-1945, the U.S. Navy Task Force 38, comprising 15 modern fast carriers and 90 other assorted ships, was joined by 28 ships of the Royal Navy off the Japanese home islands. Nineteen carriers bearing more than 1,000 aircraft began systematic raids that were dubbed the "Inland Sea air strikes." From July 24 through July 28, 1945, the attacking U.S. aircraft sank or damaged the remainder of the Imperial Japanese Navy that had attempted to hide or camouflage itself in various naval installations. Most ships were found in Kure Bay, and this area became another involuntary warship boneyard, known as the boneyard fleet of Japan. Among the 80-plus ships found immobilized at the end of the war

were three battleships (*Haruna, Ise, Nagato*), four aircraft carriers (*Katsuragi, Amagi, Ryuho, Aso*), and scores of cruisers, destroyers, submarines, and service craft. Unlike the defeated Russian squadron at Port Arthur, the German Navy in World War I, or the French Fleet at Toulon, the Japanese Fleet was annihilated by its collective enemies before it could make any attempt to scuttle.

Although warship boneyards don't originate in the same fashion as inactive fleet sites of the Allied navies in postwar environments, all share a commonality. The sunken ships at Port Arthur, Scapa Flow, Toulon, and Kure Bay were eventually raised and broken up. With a few rare exceptions, ships in reserve fleets will face the same destiny.

The frigate USS Constitution, still in active commission in the U.S. Navy, was able to move under sail power in this July 21, 1998, photograph. The 44-gun Constitution was one of the original six frigates authorized by the U.S. Congress in 1794. She was designed by Joshua Humphreys and built at Hartt's Shipyard in Boston, Massachusetts. In and out of commission many times in her over 200-year history, "Old Ironsides" is the oldest actively commissioned warship in any navy. Navy League

Chapter Two
EARLY RESERVE FLEETS

1800–1860

Agrowing sense of dissatisfaction with Great Britain and its policies of taxation led the Colonies to rebel in 1775, and by November of that year, the fledgling Continental Congress formed a 13-man Naval Committee. Of course, forming a committee would not sweep the Royal Navy from the sea, but it was a beginning. After considerable debate, two merchantmen were converted to sloops of war and armed (the *Columbus* had 20 guns and the *Alfred* had 24 guns) and an expedition was mounted to attack and loot the British garrison at Nassau in February 1776. The amphibious raid was successful and was the first and last of its type during the Revolutionary War. From that point onward, the Continental Navy changed its thrust to attacking merchantmen and avoiding British men-of-war if possible. It was joined by a number of "state navies" from Massachusetts, Connecticut, and other colonies when they could raise money, collect ships, and induce men to fight. These private navies were loyal to the cause, but more loyal to their home colony—much like local militia. Generally, they were unsuccessful except when interdicting enemy commerce at sea.

The privateer was the most successful aspect of the sea war, greatly benefiting the Colonies as a whole and forwarding their ground campaign. Greed and easy pickings caused the privateer to get to sea and attempt to capture British merchantmen despite the Royal Navy's blockade. Besides providing ready-made wealth to owners and crews, the effort had a devastating effect on British trade. During the course of the war, it was estimated that more than 2,000 American privateers were at sea and hunting for British merchant ships. In concert with the French and Spanish toward the end of the war, these ships caused the loss of 3,176 British vessels. It was not all one-sided, however, as the British captured or recaptured some 2,244 ships. On the whole, the balance sheet favored the Colonies and their new allies. For the British crown, this was a definite incentive for ending the war. Another, more-compelling reason was dealing with the French Navy, which eventually came to the aid of the new country, and with "ships of the line" broke the Royal Navy's hold.

The triumph over the Royal Navy was indeed fortunate. The untrained and vastly under-funded Continental Navy never amounted to more than 53 ships in total (1775–1783); consequently, there was no real possibility of squadron or combined fleet operations. Most of the Continental Navy's ships were effectively confined to harbors by the British blockade, and by the war's end, virtually the entire American Navy had been destroyed. The Navy's ships did capture or destroy more than 200 British merchant ships, thereby justifying the confidence of the Naval Committee and laying the foundation for what would become the United States Navy.

The signing of the Treaty of Paris in 1783 ended the war. By this time, there was only one vessel left flying the flag of the Continental Navy. It was decided to retain the sole survivor, the frigate *Alliance*, armed with 32 guns, for flag showing, but it, too, became too expensive for the new government. In 1785, she was sold, and the country was without a navy.

A month older than the USS *Constitution*, the U.S. frigate *Constellation* (38 guns) has not been as well taken care of over the years as her sister, the USS *Constitution*. The *Constellation* has found a home in Baltimore, Maryland, where she was originally launched on September 7, 1797. She, like most warships of the nineteenth century, was in one warship boneyard after another in between commissions. After being saved by President Franklin Roosevelt and serving as the relief flagship of the Atlantic Fleet during World War II, the old ship is back at Baltimore where she is being restored. *Courtesy U.S. Frigate Constellation Association*

The United States held no ships in reserve, and most of the state navies' ships had been sunk or captured by the Royal Navy. Those that survived were returned to their former pursuits or were broken up. The privateers surely regretted the end of the war, but they, too, returned to peacetime occupations. The Revolutionary War produced no warship boneyards. As to the future, the United States hoped that her commerce and shores would be trouble free, based on her distance from Europe and the goodwill of other nations. In 1786, the Barbary Pirates of the north coast of Africa buried this line of thinking less than one year after the *Alliance* was sold.

American shipping was being captured and crews were held in slavery for ransom or tribute by the Barbary Pirates. These same minor potentates paid respect to those European nations that had powerful naval forces, but realized that the United States had no warships. The alternative was to pay what amounted to protection money. Despite the pleas of George Washington to establish, build, and equip a modern navy, Congress voted in 1792 to pay off the pirates. The French Revolution intervened, however, and with it came the capture of neutral

This is the planked-over USS *Independence* at the Mare Island Naval Shipyard before it was decommissioned in 1912. There were many residents of nearby Vallejo, California, who had never known the yard to be without the elderly ship, which was the nation's first "ship of the line." The *Independence* served as a receiving ship at the Mare Island Naval Shipyard. *Treasure Island Museum*

(U.S.) shipping at sea. The issue of paying tribute became secondary to facing the problem of French warships and privateers plundering and capturing American merchant ships. So much for the goodwill of former allies.

A Reluctant Government and Its Budget Navy

By 1794, Congress yielded to the obvious need for a navy and authorized the construction of six modern, large frigates. Two of the six, the USS *Constitution* (44 guns) and the U.S. frigate *Constellation* (36 guns) survived to become memorial ships. They formed the beginning of the United States Navy, which still had many obstacles to overcome before becoming a respected fighting force.

Funding for additional ships was difficult to secure primarily due to a limited national budget, and many congressional members still felt that U.S. interests should be directed inward rather than onto the high seas. The election of the Jeffersonian party to Congress in 1800 indirectly caused the first true U.S. Navy warship boneyard. Problems with former ally France were resolved, and in 1801 the U.S. Congress passed the Peace Establishment Act, which in part provided continued funding for a minimum of 13 frigates. Six remained in active service with reduced crews.

The act also forced the retirement of seven frigates that were to be laid up "in ordinary," as well as the sale of the rest of the Navy's vessels for $300,000. Among those chosen to enter the reserve fleet were the frigates *Constitution, Constellation, United States, President, Congress,* and *Chesapeake*. The latter four were laid up on June 6, 1801, in the Potomac River adjacent to the newly built Washington Navy Yard, and the *Constitution* was moored at Charleston, South Carolina. For the first time in history, the United States had a navy to lay up

during periods of relative peace. The *Constitution* was recommissioned in late 1803 and sent to the Mediterranean to assist with the continuing Barbary Pirate difficulty. The other ships were moored in freshwater basins under the protection of skeleton crews and dockyard staff that ensured these ships remained in adequate condition should they be recalled to duty. This included periodic painting, continual leak prevention, hull cleanings, and tarring of lines. To inspect and repair the hull beneath the waterline, ships were careened over in shallow water. Although all equipment was stored ashore in warehouses, the greatest enemy of a wooden ship is not water, but sunlight. This caused planking to separate, and pitch was used to help seal planks that would harden beyond usefulness. The *United States* emerged from the Washington Navy Yard in 1810 after nearly a decade of being in a boneyard, and was rendered fighting-ready for the war with Great Britain that was to come in two years.

A pattern had emerged with these frigates and the U.S. Navy. They were built, used in active service, placed "in ordinary," recalled for national defense, and again returned to reserve status. This was due to politics and a level of appropriations so low that it was nearly impossible to maintain a satisfactory standing navy. It was true in 1800 and is still true at the beginning of the twenty-first century.

Shortly after Thomas Jefferson was elected president of the United States, he laid out naval policies that preferred coastal gunboats over a blue-water fleet. He felt that a nation without a large navy would project the very image of peace. Besides, the gunboats could be built and laid up until needed for local defense. Another scheme provided that large covered structures would be built to house the navy while it waited in reserve. Congress refused the housed dry-dock plan, but authorized the construction of 25 gunboats, and then on December 8, 1897, approved funding for an additional 188 gunboats. The total number of gunboats topped 200 before construction was ended. It was thought the additional gunboats would save an estimated $192,000 per year that was required to sustain a man-of-war at sea. The U.S. Navy, which had planned to build "ships of the line" with up to 74 guns each, watched its precious seasoned timber being used in Jefferson's gunboat scheme. The War of 1812 with Great Britain exposed "Jeffy's gunboats" for what they were—worthless. At the end of the war, the gunboat scheme caused the U.S. Congress to vote to set aside funds for four "ships of the line." Preventing American sailors from being impressed into the Royal Navy on the high sea, and protecting merchantmen from capture could not be accomplished by the one-gun-armed coastal boats. The U.S. Navy fielded 9 frigates and 8 other smaller combat ships to fight the Royal Navy, which had available 120 ships of the line and 116 frigates included in a total force of 1,048 combatants.

The USS *Hartford,* seen here shortly after the beginning of the twentieth century, was a training ship for the U.S. Navy. This heavily armed screw sloop was launched in 1858 and was a prime example of what modern mid-century warships could be. She was armed with 20 9-inch *Dahlgren* guns and gained notoriety and fame throughout her career, which ended 108 years later when she sank at her moorings at the Norfolk Navy Yard in 1956. The *Hartford* was in and out of commission, yet will always be known as Admiral D. W. Farragut's flagship at the Battle of Mobile Bay in 1864 when he yelled, "damn the torpedoes (mines), full speed ahead." *U.S.N.I.*

In this photograph taken before 1891, the USS *New Hampshire* sits at Newport, Rhode Island, where she was the flagship of Admiral Stephen B. Luce's Apprentice Training Squadron for the Navy. The *New Hampshire,* which had been the USS *Alabama,* very briefly was laid down in 1819, and was ready for launching six years later. For an additional 39 years she waited, and on April 23, 1864, the obsolete but brand-new vessel took to the water. Instead of the 74 guns that were planned in 1816, she was armed with six relatively modern heavy guns. She served her career as a stores and receiving ship until she became Admiral Luce's flagship. Her final duty after being decommissioned in 1892 was to be a training ship for the State of New York as the *Granite State. U.S.N.I.*

There were individual ship-to-ship duels, yet like déjà vu, it again was the American privateer that caused the greatest challenge to the Royal Navy during the War of 1812. There were 250 American ships armed with written American government permission, and they seized 991 British vessels. A war-weary English population was then eager for peace, and the war ended almost as abruptly as it had started. On December 24, 1814, peace terms were agreed upon.

The war caused the government to realize the value of a blue-water navy, and the ships of the line were approved. The first was the USS *Independence* (74 guns) which was the class leader. Eventually 10 more were authorized. The careers of the 14 ships of the line that were built were excellent examples of how the U.S. Navy brings ships in and out of service and occasionally maintains them in a reserve site for decades prior to official disposition. These ships clearly set the pattern of the way the ships of the U.S. Navy were to be used, which continues even to the present day.

A Pattern Is Set for the Future

The *Independence* was commissioned in 1815, and served until 1822, when she spent the next 14 years being laid up. The *Independence* went in and out of commission 11 times from 1815 until 1857. Her last cruise was from 1854 until 1857, and she became a planked-over receiving ship at the Mare Island Naval Shipyard until her sale in 1913. She far outlasted her builders and former crew, served the U.S. Navy for 98 years, and witnessed the development of modern weaponry and a standing navy. The U.S. Congress was attentive to military spending, and certainly got its money's worth from this ship, which originally cost $329,000. She was sold by the Navy for $3,515 and was towed to the mud flat of lower San Francisco Bay, where she was burned to recover copper fittings. Other ships of the line and frigates were treated similarly. The longest surviving ship of the line was the *Granite State*, ex–USS *New Hampshire*, ex–USS *Alabama*. She was built at the Portsmouth Naval Shipyard and remained on the launching platform (in stocks) from 1825 until April 23, 1864. She became obsolete and would not have been used at all had it not been for the dire need of ships in the American Civil War. She was finally launched and fitted out to aid the Union blockade of the Confederacy. At the end of the Civil War, she was used for training and as a flagship for apprentices. She was transferred to the New York State Militia and renamed the *Granite State* in 1902. On her way to the shipbreakers, the old ship inadvertently was lost as the result of a fire and a storm in July 1922. Interestingly, two other ships of the line, the intended USS *New Orleans* and USS *Chippewa* were partially built, virtually complete, and kept on stocks. Both were fitted out in 1815. The *Chippewa* remained ready for completion until 1833 when it was sold, and the *New Orleans* sat until 1883. Steel had already replaced iron as the primary medium of ship construction, and sail was a mere adjunct to the steam propulsion systems in modern warships. The *New Orleans* was likely the only brand-new ship ever to sit in a self-imposed land warship boneyard for seven decades!

The world was changing around the new nation and despite the great distances between her shores

The New York Navy Yard in 1876. Few photographic images are available of older ships laid up "in ordinary"; however, the upper background shows what appears to be four vessels with bare masts. When there was no overt threat of war, the East Coast was crowded with such ships. The wooden screw sloop USS *Swatara* sits in the foreground. *U.S.N.I.*

and that of other powerful seagoing nations, the United States was dependent on seaborne trade. Communication had improved and in this sense the world was becoming smaller. The United States would soon be forced to take its place in the international naval community. There was also the movement west that mandated that the United States would have to confront those that owned property out west such as Mexico, France, and Russia. The option seemed to be surrendering lands for a price, through diplomacy or warfare. Commercial interests and those who pioneered the West looked to their government for support. This required warships to be brought in and out of reserve for one venture after another, and it also meant that a standing navy of progressively newer ships was needed. Too often, those ships coming out of a decommissioned status were in poor condition and obsolete. The introduction of modern steam sloops and frigates of war during the 1850s relegated the older warships of the past to less important roles. One of the most outstanding of these steam sloops was the USS *Hartford*, which gained her fame at the American Civil War Battle of Mobile Bay as Admiral D. W. Farragut's flagship.

By the onset of the Civil War in 1861, most of the older vessels in the American Navy were languishing in one boneyard or another along the East Coast, having succumbed to steam-powered warships. The number of ships was not great in comparison to those in the 1920s and late 1940s, but the practice of "boneyarding" vessels had become standard operating procedure for the U.S. Navy. Some were eventually discarded, but there was a final reprieve for many—they were brought out of retirement to serve the Union cause. As the war intensified, everything that could float or be made to float was commandeered to blockade the Confederate coastline and chase down blockade runners. Westward expansion, curbing the slave trade off the Ivory Coast in Africa, flag showing, and dreams of foreign imperialism would have to take a back seat to preserving the United States from being permanently fractured. Warship boneyards were now practically empty.

A drawing of the Union Navy steam sloop USS Kearsarge under sail and steam. This vessel, commissioned January 24, 1862, was similar to that of the steam sloop USS Pawnee. The Kearsarge sank the famous Confederate raider CSS Alabama on June 19, 1864, in a spirited ship duel off the shore of Cherbourg, France. The aging Kearsarge soldiered on until February 2, 1894, when she was wrecked near South America. Ironically, the Kearsarge and other obsolete ships like her in the U.S. Naval inventory were the object of ridicule by navies around the world. Even smaller navies, such as Chile's, had built steel and heavily armed warships based on the example set by the inventions of the American Civil War. To stand still is to fall behind in naval affairs. U.S.N.I.

Chapter Three

THE AMERICAN CIVIL WAR

1861–1865

Civil wars are the bloodiest and most passionate of all wars fought. They are generally the most costly involving lives and money, and their stain is left for generations. The Civil War in the United States fought between the Confederate States of America (South) and the United States of America (North) was no different. During the four years of combat (1861–1865), the casualties amounted to more than 620,000 known dead and a similar number of missing or wounded. This total is more than the combined losses of all the wars fought by the United States in its entire history.

On April 12, 1861, President Abraham Lincoln sent the new screw sloop USS *Pawnee* (similar to the USS *Kearsarge*) with the steamship *Baltic* and a revenue cutter to re-provision and reinforce Fort Sumter in Charleston Harbor. The effort was too late, as the fort surrendered on April 13th. From that point the war began in earnest.

The Union Navy began the war with 90 ships, of which 42 were commissioned. The other 48 vessels were laid up "in ordinary," or being fitted out for commissioning. There were 23 steam-powered ships in the fleet. Fortunately, many of the steam vessels were relatively modern and armed with *Dahlgren* guns that could fire shot and exploding shells. More than 1,000 naval officers were available after those had left to join the Confederate cause. U.S. Navy Secretary Gideon Welles immediately initiated a plan to buy, build, and commandeer anything that could float and fight. All ships laid "up in ordinary" (21 vessels) were to be refurbished, re-armed, and given assignments. This included craft such as inland ferry boats with a pilothouse at either end, which could go backwards and forwards. This type of vessel was of great value in narrow rivers. Warships assigned to the Pacific and the Anti-Slavery Patrol were recalled, but this added little to the available force.

The overall plan of the North was to place a stranglehold on the South through a tight naval blockade of its coastline, while fighting its way through the Mississippi River and invading the heartland with its armies. It was appropriately code-named "Anaconda." The Confederate coastline was 3,550 miles in length, and there were 189 harbors and deep-water rivers to guard. On paper it was an excellent strategy, but first the armed forces of the Union had to be recruited and trained. The Union Navy began with 7,600 men and a massive plan for building a navy that would stand at 264 ships in commission within eight months after the Fort Sumter surrender. The Union Navy also had more than 20,000 men under arms to serve.

The South had a very limited number of smaller ships and commercial craft suitable for inland and blue-water fighting. Confederate forces did subdue the Pensacola (Florida) Navy Yard, and seized the Norfolk (Virginia) Navy Yard on April 20, 1864. They secured a graving dock, the ordnance shops, and more than 300 modern *Dahlgren* guns. This was the single largest number of modern heavy weapons in the world to date, and the South was the grateful beneficiary. Just before the Southern troops broke into the yard, Commodore Hiram Paulding arrived aboard the USS *Pawnee* and attempted to destroy the yard. He partially succeeded and sunk nine vessels and burnt the new 50-gun steam frigate USS *Merrimack* to the waterline. The *Pawnee* also was able to tow the 32-gun sloop of war, USS *Cumberland*, to safety. Four days later, the cadets and staff of the U.S. Naval Academy at Annapolis boarded the USS *Constitution* and sailed for New York. The Academy relocated to Newport, Rhode Island, for the duration of the war.

The Confederate Navy had inherited quite a find in the *Merrimack* and immediately set about rebuilding her as an ironclad floating fortress. The mission of the new vessel was the destruction of the Union blockading force, to disrupt shipping, provide support for ground forces, and lift the coastal siege of the

The USS *Lackawanna* was a typical Civil War–built steam sloop of war and had a career that lasted from 1862 up through April 1885 when she was decommissioned at the Mare Island Navy Yard. The *Lackawanna* achieved a degree of fame when she and other ships under the command of Admiral David Farragut forced their way into Mobile Bay against a Confederate squadron that included the ironclad ram CSS *Tennessee* on August 5, 1864. During the battle, the *Lackawanna* successfully rammed the *Tennessee*, which helped lead to a victory and the closure of the last major port in the South. *Vallejo Naval Museum*

A row of Civil War-built *Monitors* in reserve at League Island. Most of the *Monitors* sat for years rusting away until they were scrapped. They had been built for a war that was over and had little usefulness in future conflicts. The USS *Nahant* is shown with her stack and turret openings covered, and wooden enclosures protecting entry ports. After 33 years of sitting in reserve, the old *Monitor* was recommissioned to protect New York harbor during the Spanish-American War. She was finally sold in 1904. *U.S. Navy*

upon first meeting the USS *Cumberland*, rammed her, and then shot her to pieces. The hapless *Cumberland* settled to the bottom. The *Virginia*'s next victim was the USS *Congress*, a 50-gun steam frigate and sister to the former USS *Merrimack*. The *Congress* was shot up so badly that she became a fiery wreck and surrendered. With the loss of daylight, and the next target, the 50-gun steam frigate USS *Minnesota* (also a sister to the *Congress*), grounded beyond effective gun range, the *Virginia* left the area. It planned to return the following day and dispatch the balance of the blockading force.

On March 9, 1862, an unusual-looking warship sat waiting near the stranded *Minnesota* for the arrival of the *Virginia*. The John Ericsson-designed and -built USS *Monitor* had been hurriedly sent to protect the blockading force. The *Virginia* was revolutionary, but far less inventive than the *Monitor*. This new ship had a movable turret and was low to the water—"cheese box on a raft." When the two odd-looking warships met, a shooting duel ensued that ended late in the afternoon. Technically, the outcome was a draw. In reality, the *Virginia* was driven off by the diminutive *Monitor*, and the blockading squadron was preserved, including the still-grounded *Minnesota*. The *Virginia* was sufficiently damaged to require dry-docking, while her opponent suffered only superficial damage. There was no rematch, and both vessels were eventually lost in noncombat incidents—later in 1862, the *Virginia* was blown up to avoid capture, and the USS *Monitor* foundered in a storm. Foreign naval observers saw the battle for what it was—the end of an era and the dawn of a new phase of naval warfare.

The Union and Confederate Navies continued to build ironclads and armored ships during the war. The South preferred the design of the *Virginia* and the North did not stray far from Ericsson's *Monitor*. By the end of the war, 74 *Monitor*-class ships had been built—many with two turrets, and the USS *Roanoke* had three turrets. The *Roanoke* was special in that she was once a sister to the *Merrimack*, and

South. The South recognized that it could never compete with the North in warship construction, so it chose audacity and inventiveness as an equalizer. It developed mines, torpedoes, and submarines. The most memorable engagement was the night attack of the armed submersible (CSS *H. L. Hunley*) against the Union blockader USS *Housatonic* on February 17, 1864. It was a surface attack, but the Union warship was lost nevertheless along with her attacker.

As to the first ironclad in the Americas, the Confederate Navy conferred upon the new ship the name CSS *Virginia*, but for most Americans, the ship will always be known as the *Merrimack*. It was not long before the secret monster being built in the South revealed itself to the public. On March 8, 1862, the CSS *Virginia*, known as the "barn," steamed down the Elizabeth River into what could be described as a massive water arena—Hampton Roads, where she met the sole escapee from the Norfolk Navy Yard—the sail-powered 32-gun sloop USS *Cumberland*. The shoreline was lined with spectators from all over the world to watch what an ironclad could achieve in combat. The *Virginia*,

The USS *Saugus* was a single-turret *Monitor* that had a varied career throughout the Civil War and served at a number of naval stations in the Atlantic and Caribbean. She was eventually decommissioned for the last time on October 8, 1877. She sat at the Washington Navy Yard until 1886 when she was condemned and sold. During her stint at the Washington Navy Yard, she was preserved like all vessels of that day with the technology available. Interior spaces were sealed and entry ports to the hull were closed and greased. *U.S.N.I.*

like the South had done, the Union Navy built an ironclad over her razed hull. The South built or out-fitted nearly 40 ironclads, mostly for inland water work, but all were destroyed during the war.

Similar to the Continental Navy during the Revolutionary War, the Confederacy resorted to pri-vateering; however, the Union blockade and its blue-water warships prevented any substantial use of this tactic. Blockade running became a more popular method of gaining the open sea and returning to Southern ports laden with European goods. The lure to run the blockade was somewhat romantic, often profitable, and always dangerous. Union cruisers shot to kill and sink.

The Union Navy was particularly mindful of the Gulf Coast of the Confederacy, and in one of the most spirited battles of the Civil War, Admiral D. W. Farragut attacked the defenders at Mobile Bay, Alabama. He chose the redoubtable screw sloop USS *Hartford* as his flagship, and on August 5, 1864, forced his way into the bay against torpedo mines, shore batteries, and the Confederate ironclad CSS *Tennessee*. By the end of the day the Confederate forces surrendered, and the last port on the Gulf coast was closed.

By 1865, the Union Navy was successful in pre-venting all but a trickle of trade in and out of Southern ports, through its inshore blockade and after capturing several Confederate harbors. The "Anaconda Plan" worked once the U.S. Navy had a sufficiency of warships to guard the coastal areas. On April 9, 1865, Confederate General Robert E. Lee surrendered to Union General U. S. Grant, but it was not until November 5th that the last Southern raider, the CSS *Shenandoah*, hauled down the "Stars and Bars" in Liverpool, England. The ship had been out of land communication for four months.

The war at sea during the American Civil War was fought primarily in coastal waters and within the confines of most of the major rivers of the divided countries. The Union Navy ended the war with some 700 ships flying the Stars and Stripes, and most of the 500 Confederate or private naval vessels of the South were sunk, burned, or damaged beyond repair. With the war over, the reunited country turned its priority toward reconstruction. Domestic issues far outweighed funding requests for maintaining a large fleet at sea, let alone inactive vessel preservation or research and development of naval science.

The U.S. Navy in Post–Civil War Decline

The United States Navy of 1865 was one of the most powerful and modern in the world. But besides having just large numbers, the Navy had also made strides in naval tactics and technology. The Union and Confederate Navies had developed and tested the torpedo boat and submersibles, and made more effective use of mine warfare. Armored steam-pow-ered frigates with innovations copied from Ericsson's *Monitor* produced what amounted to the immediate precursor to the modern battleship. She was the 373-foot-long *Dunderberg*, a huge steam-powered ironclad frigate that mounted two revolving gun casemates and broadside guns. Due to cutbacks in naval spending, she was never commissioned into the U.S. Navy and eventually was sold to France, where she served as the *Rochambeau*.

The uncompleted *Dunderberg* was not the only victim of postwar cost consciousness. By the end of 1866, 400 of the U.S. Navy's blockading ships had been sold off or scrapped, and three years later only 52 vessels were in full commission. Most of these were quickly obsolescing compared to other warships in the international naval community. The U.S. government chose to redirect tax dollars to other pursuits and place most of its ships "in ordinary" up one river or another.

Monitors such as the USS *Nahant* had fought in one engagement after another on the East Coast and now were placed in reserve at League Island (Philadelphia Navy Yard). Many remained to rust at their moorings for decades until being recalled for service for minor support roles in the Spanish-American War in 1898. Typically, ex-Civil War veterans were kept in freshwater basins such as League Island on the Delaware River. The ships were tied up to available piers where active ships were not moored or along the banks of the rivers. The sail-powered vessels were placed "in ordinary" much the same as before the war; however, the steam-powered ships were treated with certain differences.

The engineering plants of the steam-powered warships had to be protected from corrosion, but there was little knowledge available on this subject during the immediate years following the Civil War. Engineering spaces were kept reasonably dry, and moving parts were greased and operated on a periodic basis. Ship custodians occasionally inspected the decommissioned vessels to prevent vandalism and theft as well as ensuring their charges were still afloat.

The ironclads were treated in much the same manner except each hatch and access port was closed or covered with wood or canvas. Ventilators and funnels were sealed to keep inclement weather out, and wooden structures were built over large deck apertures. This was a crude beginning to the future of sophisticated inactive ship maintenance. At various times, ships were brought out of storage for recommissioning, and it was still far less expensive to refit an existing ship than to build a new vessel. This was not the most beneficial method of providing national defense at sea. Refitting old ships and continued repair of existing vessels was to have an adverse effect on the development of the U.S. Navy in the post–Civil War years. These became known as the dark ages of the U.S. Navy.

The seagoing *Monitor*, the USS *Wyoming*. The *Wyoming* reflected the mindset of post–Civil War national defense—to defend the coastline and keep foreign entanglements to a minimum. This vessel was a portable coast artillery battery and could survive in the open sea, but it took green water over the bow in San Francisco Bay. In 1908 she was the first vessel in the U.S. Navy to be refitted to burn oil rather than coal. The experiment was successful and led to coal-fired boilers being phased out. Not long after the experiment, she was renamed the USS *Cheyenne* and operated as a submarine tender. She was finally decommissioned on January 25, 1937. The navy got its money's worth with this ship! *Treasure Island Museum*

An aerial view of the red lead fleet at the Philadelphia Navy Yard prior to World War II. At that time, the inactive fleet included submarines (upper left), small craft, and cargo vessels (middle right). At the far upper right is the USS *Olympia* of Spanish-American War fame. Most of the inhabitants are flush deckers that nearly 20 years after World War I still crowd the anchorage. Several of the destroyers were recalled for duty with the fleet, and 50 were selected for transfer to Great Britain and Canada in 1940. *Treasure Island Museum*

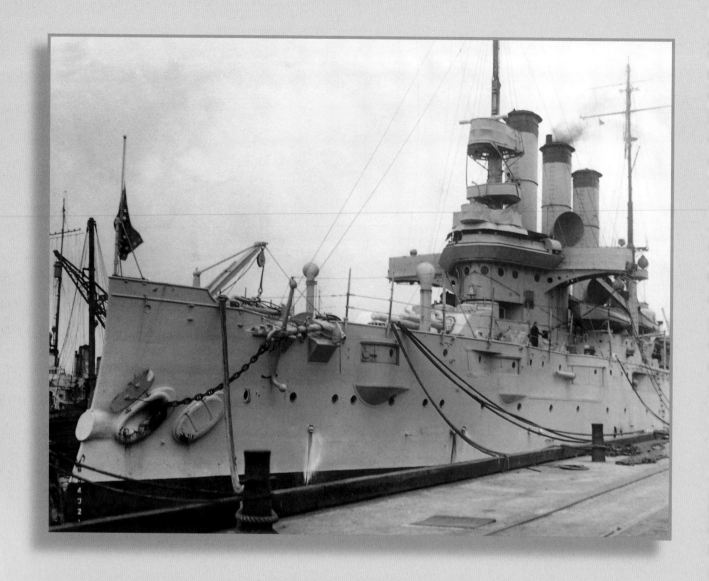

The USS Rochester (ACR-2) (ex-USS Saratoga and ex-USS New York) was moored at the Brooklyn Navy Yard in February 1927 after service off Nicaragua. As the USS New York, the 8,150-ton cruiser fought valiantly in the Spanish-American War at the Battle of Santiago Bay. The New York/Rochester was an example of the U.S. Navy's conversion to the steel navy with blue water combatants that were comparable to European navies. The old decommissioned cruiser ended her days in Olongapo Shipyard at the Philippine Islands, where she was scuttled in December 1941 to avoid Japanese capture. Author's collection

Chapter Four

THE SPANISH-AMERICAN WAR

1898

In 1881, there were some Pacific coastal nations in South America that had more-powerful naval forces than the United States. The U.S. Navy had become an embarrassment, and a renaissance in naval thinking and commitment was in order if the United States had hopes of becoming a world-class nation. President James A. Garfield supported the reconstruction of the U.S. Navy, and Congress was persuaded to agree. At first, the Navy wanted small wooden cruisers, but a vocal minority including Benjamin Isherwood (proponent and designer of the USS *Wampanoag*) forced the issue, and the ABCD (*Atlanta, Boston, Chicago, Dolphin*) ships were approved. In 1883 the

Another veteran of the Spanish-American War was the USS *Olympia*, flagship of Admiral George Dewey. Dewey's squadron entered Manila Bay on May 1, 1898, located the Spanish naval opposition, and shot it to pieces. The Philippines then became a U.S. possession. The *Olympia* served in World War I and was decommissioned at the Philadelphia Navy Yard on June 30, 1931. She is shown in this September 1957 photograph as she was pushed to her new home in Philadelphia. She was still painted navy gray from her days in the warship boneyard at the Philadelphia Navy Yard. *Treasure Island Museum–SFCB*

the steel-protected sail/steam cruisers, USS *Atlanta*, USS *Boston*, USS *Chicago*, and dispatch-communication ship USS *Dolphin* were authorized. Within six years they were on active service, and the steel navy was born.

The introduction of steel warships did not come without some sacrifice. The multitude of shipyards on the East Coast had to be consolidated, and older vessels in reserve or in commission had to be eliminated. Congress declared in no uncertain terms, that no more than 30 percent of a new ship's cost could be spent on repair or refurbishment of existing ships. This put a damper on the past practice of maintaining obsolete ships in the fleet, and inter-

rupted what had been a steady supply of "congressional pork" (congress members spending excessive amounts of money in their districts for "pet" projects) to districts where superfluous shipyards were located. Many ships were consigned to the backwaters to join other ex-Civil War notables that had been languishing for years. Several others were sent to the shipbreakers.

The *ABCD* ships led the way to more and better-protected cruisers and battleships. By the 1890s, sail gave way to steam and with that, the U.S. Navy was on the path to becoming a world-class fighting force. Congress and the people of the United States still believed in national defense by isolation, but the world was getting smaller by the year. A strong navy would guarantee that American citizens were respected abroad and commerce was protected. The overt feeling of defending the coast of the United States was still paramount in the minds of many government leaders and for that purpose "coastal battleships" and larger,

more seaworthy monitors were built. In any type of sea including the placid waters near the Mare Island Navy Yard, the most stable monitor buried its nose in the water and closely resembled a squat submarine with heavy guns. These new monitors were more like coast artillery afloat rather than ships and most ended up as submarine tenders or station ships. More far-sighted naval leaders knew that the new navy would have to venture far from coastal waters to protect the interests of the United States. For this reason, ocean-going cruisers and battleships as well as smaller combatants were being continuously introduced to the fleet. The first major test of this new and unblooded navy was to be in 1898 in Manila Bay and off Cuba. The 6,700-ton second-class battleship USS *Maine* mysteriously sank by an explosion at her moorings in Havana Harbor on February 15, 1898.

The Spanish-American War: "A Splendid Little War"

The war with Spain was ostensibly fought to prevent continued oppression of the Cuban people by the resident Spanish government. In reality it was the coming of age of the United States and its naval power. The loss of the *Maine*, even under mysterious conditions, provided a rallying point, "Remember the *Maine* and the hell with Spain." The Eastern press, led by William Randolph Hearst, fanned the incident into a war that Spain vigorously attempted to avoid. Spain declared war on the United States on April 24, 1898, and the United States obliged on the following day. What followed were a series of battles fought in the Philippines and Cuba. The war lasted until August 12, 1898, when a peace protocol was signed.

Spain was in control of the Philippine Islands when the war broke out, and the Spanish naval forces were concentrated in Manila Bay. Naval forces of the United States in the Far East (U.S. Pacific Squadron) were under the control of Commodore George Dewey aboard his flagship, the 5,900-ton protected cruiser USS *Olympia*. He had

Mare Island Navy Yard in late 1923. A number of warships await their turn to be towed to the shipbreakers. This was called "rotten row" and included the battleships *Georgia, Nebraska, Vermont,* and *Rhode Island* (right center). All were alumni of the Great White Fleet, which had made its famous cruise just 14 years earlier. They were also victims of the terms of the Washington Naval Disarmament Treaty agreed upon in 1922. To avoid scrapping newer battleships, the old ones had to go. Also shown are two older cruisers (left), and the tanker USS *Tippecanoe* (AO-21). The *Tippecanoe,* launched on June 5, 1920, went on to serve in World War II. *Vallejo Naval Museum*

The USS *Olympia* (CA-6) is shown at her permanent berth in Philadelphia alongside the GUPPY converted submarine USS *Becuna* (SS-319) in this November 15, 1999, photograph. The *Becuna* was upgraded and modernized from a *Balao*-class attack submarine to have greater underwater propulsion in 1950 and 1951. She earned four battle stars during World War II, and served in the Korean Conflict and Vietnam War. She was decommissioned on November 7, 1969, and seven years later, was rescued from a warship boneyard as a memorial boat moored next to the *Olympia*. The *Olympia* is outfitted and painted in the same manner as when she entered Manila Bay over a century ago. *Author's collection*

41

The battleship USS *Nebraska* (BB-14) was a Great White Fleet veteran, but is not sporting her peaceful colors in this pre–World War I image. This 16,000-ton battleship was armed with four 12-inch guns with eight 8-inch guns in a secondary battery. Four of the 8-inch guns were situated in twin mounts over the 12-inch gun turrets. This was a relatively new way of situating weapons and it became widely copied in the future. *Treasure Island Museum*

been directed to sail from Hawaii to Hong Kong by Assistant Secretary of the Navy Theodore Roosevelt and have the ship fully coaled pending further instructions. On May 1, 1898, Dewey entered Manila Bay with four protected cruisers (including the USS *Boston* the "B" of the *ABCD* ships of the 1880s) and three lesser vessels. Avoiding mines and shore battery fire, Dewey's ships went straight for the anchored Spanish fleet. By noon, Dewey's squadron had reduced the Spanish ships to burning rubble. The accuracy of American gunfire (4 percent) left much to be desired, but nevertheless, a great victory had taken place.

Despite the American victory in Manila Bay, there was still a grave concern that Spain would send her fleet to make hit-and-run attacks on American cities on the East Coast. *Monitors* and other combatants dating back to the Civil War that had been left to rot were hurriedly brought out of retirement and detailed to protect critical harbors in the North. In actuality, there was nothing to fear. Spain wanted out of the war nearly as much as the United States wanted into it.

The Navy needed ships to provide support to its combatants as well as transports for troops and equipment being sent to fight the ground war in Cuba. For this purpose, 50 local steamers were immediately chartered. Just simply transporting ground forces that amounted to 17,000 troops proved difficult, especially in the limited time requested. During the course of the short war, other steamers and liners were chartered for scouting work as well.

The battleship USS *Nevada* (BB-36) was commissioned on March 11, 1916, and was one of the new breed of battleships that were no longer dependent on coal. She and sister ship USS *Oklahoma* (BB-37) had oil-fired boilers and a revolutionary new approach to armor protection. The "all-or-nothing" concept of heavily protecting vital areas (turrets, magazines, engineering, conning tower) and using lesser armor on other areas was introduced in these two sister ships. This distinct trend in protection worked well in ship-to-ship duels, but was of little value against the weapons of the future—air- and submarine-launched torpedoes and armor-piercing bombs. Later, as an afterthought, these ships were armed with meager antiaircraft weaponry. The *Oklahoma* lasted a mere 20 minutes after being hit by at least eight torpedoes launched by Japanese *"Kate"* torpedo bombers during the initial stage of the December 7, 1941, Japanese air attack on Pearl Harbor. *Author's collection*

One of the most famous of all photographs of "red lead row" was this photo taken in late 1929 at the San Diego Destroyer Base. The outboard destroyer is the USS *Gillis* (DD-260) which arrived in May 1922 and remained until June 28, 1940. She was then converted to a seaplane tender AVD-12 and had a varied career throughout World War II. The *Gillis* and her sisters had been laid up for seven years when this photo was taken and red lead is showing through the peeling light gray paint on the hull and superstructure. *U.S. Navy*

The U.S. Navy eventually gathered much of its North Atlantic Squadron off Santiago Bay in early July 1898 for a showdown with the Spanish Navy. Spain fielded four older armored cruisers and two destroyers, which, during a running gun battle with U.S. battleships and cruisers, were annihilated. Augmented by the battleship USS *Oregon* (BB-3), which sailed an amazing 14,700 miles in 67 days, and ships like the 8-inch-gun armored cruiser USS *New York* (later USS *Rochester*), the Battle of Santiago Bay, fought on July 3, 1898, was a banner day for the U.S. Navy. Within days the United States won the ground campaign in Cuba, and the war was over. The war came and went so quickly that many ships in the midst of being reconditioned for combat out of the boneyards were returned back to waste away again. A few of the modern ships were placed in reserve with the exception of those that had blue-water capability.

The lessons from what diplomat John Hay, described as a "splendid little war" were simple and patently obvious. The full-time Navy was here to stay and would be vital in defending the nation and its interests. This was especially true as the United States became increasingly entangled in foreign affairs. The Spanish Navy that was so easily defeated was a rotten, foul-bottomed collection of ominous-looking vessels. The ships were old and composed of a dangerous mixture of wood and steel—an unpleasant reminder of what the U.S. Navy might have been had it not been for farsighted naval-minded supporters in the 1880s. The development of the American steel Navy allowed for a victory over the Spanish cardboard fleet. Of course, the future of the U.S. Navy now depended on the development for improved accuracy in gunnery weapons, fleet train support, regular supplies of coal, and improved amphibious capability. The U.S. Navy at the dawn of the twentieth century had a great deal of catching up to do in the world naval community.

With the help of its most famous soldier, veteran, colonel, and later president, Theodore Roosevelt, the navy continued with a program of battleship and cruiser development, supplemented by destroyers and submarines, with funds appropriated during the Spanish-American War.

Older pre–World War I destroyers of the *"flivver"* and *"thousand tonner"* classes join with scores of *Wickes/Clemson*-class flush deckers at the inactive fleet site located at the Philadelphia Navy Yard in this October 27, 1927, photograph. This was the largest warship boneyard on the East Coast and the ships literally jammed every pier. The third ship outboard from the pier (lower right) appears to be the USS *Sterett* (DD-27), with three funnels rather than four. Most of the pre–World War I vessels were stricken and broken up within a few years after this photo. *U.S.N.I.*

The "red lead row" at the Philadelphia Navy Yard in May 1936. Many of its occupants had long since been scrapped, yet several remained, including the USS Lardner (DD-286) and the USS Maury (DD-100). Both had been stricken in 1930 and were systematically being cannibalized by active units for parts. U.S.N.I.

Chapter Five

WORLD WAR I

1914–1918

The end of the Spanish-American War thrust the United States into the position of being a world power. It was to be at least a generation before naval aviation and the submarine were to be recognized for their potential. Consequently, the measure of a seafaring nation was in the strength of its battle line. In the decade preceding the Spanish-American War, the U.S. Navy embarked on a plan to develop and build increasingly powerful battleships. This trend continued through World War I and on into the first half of the twentieth century. In 1890, federal expenditures for the Navy amounted to slightly more than $22 million, or 7 percent of the federal budget. The amount had nearly tripled by 1902, with spending for naval operations, at a healthy $60.5 million or 11.3 percent of the federal budget. By the outset of World War I in Europe, the total was an astronomical $139.7 million, or 19 percent. Congressional members and leading naval officers from the post–Civil War years must have been spinning in their graves.

President Theodore Roosevelt was so proud of his new navy that, in a brash move, he decided to show it to the world. The 16-battleship voyage around the world by the "Great White Fleet" from December 1907 through February 1909 included the USS *Illinois*, USS *Vermont*, USS *Nebraska*, and the USS *Georgia*, to name a few. It clearly showed that the United States possessed a world-class navy and could venture anywhere it chose, including to Imperial Japan and across the Atlantic to European ports. This demonstration was not lost on the Japanese, who were coming to recognize that the United States would someday interfere in their plans of colonial expansion.

The dependence on the battleship for national power protection became fashionable for all nations in the world naval community. With Great Britain and France in the forefront, each nation sought to design, build, and introduce battleships that guaranteed national survival and protected its imperialism. Japan and the United States as well some South American countries joined in the battleship armament race. By the beginning of World War I in August 1914, the United States and other powers were quickly building battleship classes that successively superseded one another in technological improvements, armor thickness, and armament. This practice had a definite downside, with new classes being built before earlier ones were properly tested and had their deficiencies corrected.

From crude beginnings in 1895 with the 6,315-ton USS *San Marcos* (ex–USS *Texas*) up through the 58,000-ton *Iowa* class in World War II, the U.S. Navy

October 28, 1927, was Navy Day in San Diego, California. The tender USS *Melville* (AD-2) has *Destroyer Division 35* alongside and all are flying full colors. From left to right are the USS *MacDonough* (DD-331), USS *Mervine* (DD-322), USS *Marcus* (DD-321), USS *Mullany* (DD-325), USS *Chase* (DD-323), USS *Robert Smith* (DD-324), and USS *Selfridge* (DD-320). Thirty months later, these misleadingly attractive ships and 27 others in the Pacific Fleet would be paired off with inhabitants of red lead row. The next step for these beautiful but worn-out destroyers was the scrap heap. *Author's collection*

completed 58 battleships in at least two dozen distinct classes. One such capital ship was the USS *Michigan* (BB-27), commissioned on January 4, 1910. She was the first all-big-gun warship—with eight 12-inch/45 caliber guns—in the U.S. Navy. She and her sister, the USS *South Carolina* (BB-26), were first designed in 1904, and predated the famous British all-big-gun battleship HMS *Dreadnought*. Four years later, the USS *Texas* (BB-35) and USS *New York* (BB-34) were the most powerful battleships in the world, each mounting 10 14-inch/.45-caliber guns. The U.S. Navy had come quite a distance since the turn of the century.

One of the most important changes in the battleship and in other warships in the early twentieth century was the conversion from coal- to oil-fired boilers. In a twist of fate, the U.S. Navy's modern oil-fired battleships (*Oklahoma* and *Nevada*) were retained for service near the U.S. coastline, while the older, coal-dependent ships (USS *Delaware* and USS *Florida*) joined with the Royal Navy in the North Sea Patrol. Fuel oil was still a precious commodity in England and coal was plentiful. In 1916, when the USS *Nevada* (BB-36) and sister ship USS *Oklahoma* (BB-37) went

Sailors repair standing rigging aboard one of the red lead fleet flush deckers selected for rejuvenation in the spring of 1930. The 4-inch/.50-caliber deck gun in the background gleams with polish. The ship alongside is one that was slated for the scrapyard, and was later towed from the San Diego Destroyer Base to Mare Island for disposal. The work done by the fleet with no additional allocated funds from the U.S. Congress was nothing less than a magnificent tribute to the American seaman. Many of these ships would go on to fight in World War II, and were often in the thick of battle. *U.S. Navy*

into active service, the "all-or-nothing" concept of armor protection became standard with these ships. Vital areas such as the engineering spaces, magazines, and conning tower were heavily protected with thick armor. Other areas not considered essential to keep the ship fighting were lightly armored.

Aside from building battleships, in 1916 the U.S. Congress approved and funded the construction of submarines, torpedo boats, and destroyers to exterminate these new threats. An aggregate of 800,000 tons of naval shipping was approved, including 10 battleships, 6 battlecruisers, 10 scout cruisers, 50 destroyers, and 67 submarines. This ambitious building program still did not keep pace with international events. By the U.S. entry into World War I on April 6, 1917, the Navy had 67 destroyers; several armored, protected, and scout cruisers; and a number of elderly *Monitors* and wooden steamships, in addition to a growing number of auxiliaries. Many were unserviceable, in reserve, or stricken, and there was a severe shortage of personnel. The U.S. Navy was not yet a leader in international naval affairs. Having a series of progressively better battleships under construction may have been a boon to national prestige; however, tactics and technology were rapidly changing. The sheer power and majesty of the battleship and other major surface ships were not appropriate nor sufficient for the new type of war being waged in the Atlantic.

German U-boats manned by intrepid crews were wreaking absolute havoc with the Allies by attempting to break the British blockade. They sank merchantmen

This is the USS *Paul Hamilton* (DD-307) before she was traded in for a sister ship with lower mileage. Here the flush deck destroyer sits out of water, and sea growth covers the hull, struts, propellers, and rudder. This fouling could reduce speed by several knots. The gun on the aft deck was a 3-inch/.23-caliber antiaircraft weapon. When the *Paul Hamilton* was commissioned in September 1920, the threat of aircraft was minimal and so was this ship's original AA defense. *Treasure Island Museum*

as well as large-size warships. The Allies were desperate for men and supplies from the United States, which could easily be required from its emerging industrial output. Ships had to cross the Atlantic to bring supplies and equipment to the battlefields, and they had to be protected from submarine attack as well as German surface raiders. Ironically, the handbook for World War II and the Cold War was being written as early as 1917.

Ships that had rusted away in storage were refitted, painted, and adapted for escort duty on coastal and trans-Atlantic convoys. Monitors were used as tenders or station ships, and armored cruisers from the Spanish-American War found themselves back in commission. As had become standing procedure, ships were placed in and out of commission based on need and funding availability. One such vessel was the victor of the Battle of Manila Bay, the USS *Olympia*. The now obsolete cruiser was used for midshipman cruises, but as it became evident that the United

States would be involved in the war, the *Olympia* was used in more important roles. In 1917, she became the flagship of the North Atlantic Patrol Force and provided convoy escort services off Nova Scotia.

Her most significant role during the war was to bring back the remains of the Unknown Soldier from France. She arrived in the United States on November 9, 1921, and fired the final salute to the soldier who is known but to God, yet whose sacrifice is known to all mankind. The Great White Fleet veteran battleship USS *Nebraska* (BB-14) acted in a number of roles, including fast convoy escort. Neither the *Olympia, Nebraska*, nor many other older warships that were pressed into convoy duty were equipped to locate and sink U-boats. While the battleship remained supreme, there was a crying need for antisubmarine warfare (ASW) vessels.

As the war seemed to drag on, it became evident that the preplanned and widely anticipated duel between the Allied and German navies would not

The USS *Roper* (DD-147), USS *Elliot* (DD-146), and a sister flush decker are alongside a pier on the San Francisco waterfront shortly after being rebuilt at the Mare Island Navy Yard in 1930. They look quite different than the year before, when they were dirty and unkempt ships in red lead row. The *Roper* had a stellar career during World War II that included sinking the German U-boat *U-85* off North Carolina in May 1942. She was converted to an APD (fast transport) and fought in the Mediterranean, and in the closing days of the war was hit by a kamikaze off Japan. The *Elliot* fought in the Aleutians during World War II and was converted to a high-speed minesweeper (DSM). Both ships were decommissioned and sold shortly after the end of World War II. *Author's collection*

"Red lead row" at the San Diego Destroyer Base. This is where most of the inactivated flush deck destroyers rested. Six ships up from the bottom are two *Eagle Boats* sandwiched in among the flush deckers. From here came the replacements in 1930 for the 34 destroyers that were worn out. Visible are the USS *Walker* (DD-163), USS *O'Bannion* (DD-177), and USS *Howard* (DD-179) (far back). All were decommissioned in 1922 and never resurrected for further service. All were stricken in the late 1930s. *Treasure Island Museum*

extend beyond the Battle of Jutland fought on May 31, 1916. The grand specter of mile upon mile of parallel lines of battleships and battlecruisers firing at one another, with light cruisers and destroyers making pinprick attacks with torpedoes and smaller caliber guns, was not to be. Even the Battle of Jutland, which pitted the Royal Navy's Grand Fleet against the German High Seas Fleet, did not measure up to the illusion that was continuously in the mind's eye of naval leaders on both sides.

Naval warfare in the Atlantic during World War I was a type that ensured that men and war materiel arrived safely to Allied ports, and that Germany and its allies were effectively blockaded. Germany also announced its own naval blockade of Great Britain and the Allies. This translated to submarines, commerce raiding cruisers, and destroyers. It also meant that cargo vessels could form a "water bridge" for men and materiel from the United States to Great Britain. By 1922, a total of 2,316 ships of varying tonnage were built in the United States for this purpose. Most were constructed of steel and iron, but some 400 in the 3,000–4,000-ton displacement range were built of wood. Desperately searching for any material suitable for ship construction, American naval architects even chose steel mesh-reinforced concrete. All made the contribution necessary to

transport 800,000 men and millions of supplies and equipment to Europe for the war effort.

Aside from the thousands of ships built for transportation, various shipyards in the United States were turning out what was most vital—ASW ships. Antisubmarine warfare was quite crude, and although listening devices (e.g., hydrophones) were in their infant use, visual location of a periscope or a telltale underwater shadow was the most efficient means of sighting an enemy submarine. Keeping the U-boat submerged through the use of concentrated ASW escorts hampered its mobility and allowed many a convoy to safely elude attack. In order to accomplish this, a large number of escorts was required, and the United States agreed to provide them.

Contracts were signed for 267 *Wickes/Clemson*-class flush-deck, four-stack destroyers, which displaced 1,150 tons and had four 4-inch/.50-caliber guns. These ships, designed in 1916, also carried depth charges for ASW work and 12 21-inch torpedo tubes. Added to these were 60 *Eagle Boats* (PE) and 340 wooden-hulled submarine chasers (SC) used for escort work. The war ended on November 11, 1918, with the signing of the armistice. The formal end of hostilities caught the shipyards unaware, stuck with hundreds of uncompleted ships that were no longer necessary to the war effort. Destroyer production continued, although many were sailed directly to reserve fleet bastions.

The U.S. Navy, which had once coveted the stature of a fighting force second only to Great Britain, had vowed at the beginning of the war to have a navy second to none. Unfortunately, the building program approved by the U.S. Congress in 1916 and further augmented during the war years produced the size of navy that was desired, but the abrupt end of the war caused an overabundance of smaller naval vessels and auxiliaries. To this number, over 2,000 transport and cargo ships were added that eventually exacerbated a worldwide shipping glut. In less than five years, the industrial output of the United States produced a phenomenal number of warships and merchant vessels. The end of the war resulted in the largest warship boneyards that had never been seen before. The Philadelphia and San Diego Navy Yards were two of the largest storage sites, and most other naval bases had varying numbers of ships held in reserve. The U.S. Navy was now comparable to its mentor, the Royal Navy, but the majority of its ships were "cold iron" and moored in newly created warship boneyards. The usual postwar funding cuts consigned most of the fleet (exclusive of the more modern battleships) to inactive status.

The Interwar Years and "Red Lead Row"

In the early years following the armistice, the Navy was compelled to divert most of its scarce funding to maintaining its battleships, upon which it still believed the safety of the nation depended. After disposing of many of the very elderly production destroyers, the U.S. Navy had a destroyer force of 319 vessels. With allotted funding, there was little chance of maintaining this number on active status. Many of the new destroyers and *Eagle Boats* were decommissioned by late 1922, and joined dozens of other inactive ships. Rust spots on the superstructures and lower hulls were routinely painted with red lead paint to inhibit corrosion. The paint stood out, and the rows of inactive ships became collectively identified as "red lead row"—the name stuck for nearly two decades. Aside from the large numbers of chronologically new warships that went into reserve in 1922 due to budget cuts, the Naval Armament Limitation Treaty signed on February 6, 1922, in Washington, D.C., resulted in the inactivation and scrapping of several vessels. The list contained some famous names of older battleships.

Destroyers were towed to the Mare Island Navy Yard in early 1930 to be refitted for service as part of the overall destroyer replacement program. In less than six months, these and other rebuilt destroyers with the crews that worked on them were back in the fleet. In the far distance is the USS *Lea* (DD-118), and the sixth ship inboard is the USS *Elliot* (DD-146). Another destroyer in this group is the USS *Buchanan* (DD-131), which was refurbished and traded to Great Britain in the "bases for destroyers" deal in September 1940. As the *H.M.S. Campbeltown,* she was the lead ship on the March 28, 1942, St. Nazaire raid. She was driven up on the locks of a major dock and 11 hours later, her 5 tons of explosives wreaked havoc on the entire shipyard area as well as killing a number of German observers. *Vallejo Naval Museum*

In 1921, at the request of the Warren G. Harding administration, representatives of the United States, Great Britain, Italy, France, and Japan met in Washington, D.C., to hammer out a naval arms limitation treaty. The primary focus was on the construction and number of capital ships allowed per nation. The aircraft carrier and submarine were still considered secondary weapons. A formula was agreed upon where the U.S. Navy and Great Britain's Royal Navy were allowed an aggregate of 525,000 tons of combatants. France and Italy were allowed 175,000 tons, and Japan was limited to 315,000 tons. There were further restrictions as to the size of weapons and tonnage per vessel, but in essence, the treaty was designed to slow down the growth of navies and thus reduce the possibility of war. The United States scrapped 17 of its older vessels including the USS *Vermont,* USS *Georgia,* and USS *Rhode Island,* and broke up several new battleships that were on the builders' ways, such as the USS *Montana* at Mare Island Naval Shipyard. Older battleships, the USS *Oregon* and USS *Illinois,* were spared as long as they served in a noncombatant role. The Washington Naval Arms Limitation Treaty, and subsequent attempts in 1930 and 1936 to curb naval expansion, had a telling affect on the U.S. Navy's warship boneyards.

During the immediate years following the war and the implementation of the Naval Treaty, the U.S. Navy at first attempted to maintain 152 destroyers in active service. This meant rotating crews among ships or operating vessels with up to 20 percent fewer crewmen. Fuel oil was rationed and spare parts were difficult to find or have manufactured. This plan was ideal, but not practical. More and more ships found their way into inactive fleet maintenance sites. By 1926, the San Diego Destroyer Base played host to 76 inactive flush deck destroyers, as well as *Eagle Boats* and auxiliaries. Mare Island's boneyard sported a large number of flush deck destroyers and more than a dozen *Eagle Boats.* By 1923, its famous "rotten row" was composed of several older battleships that were headed for the scrap yard. By 1926, the Philadelphia Navy Yard had 85 inactive flush deck destroyers that were moored bow to stern crowding its piers. Older colliers and cargo vessels were also moored, awaiting disposition.

As destroyers became worn beyond usefulness, they were exchanged for those that sat in "red lead rows." The used-up vessels were scrapped, providing tonnage available for new construction under the terms of the treaties and their subsequent amendments.

The methods used to preserve ships in "red lead rows" consisted of guarding them from vandalism and theft through the use of civilian caretakers (often retired naval personnel) and protecting the ships from the elements. Hatches were sealed and interior spaces were kept reasonably dry with pans of unslaked lime lying in each sealed compartment. The pans were periodically replaced by base personnel, and staff scraped and painted the ships' outside surfaces. All moving parts and machinery were well oiled and greased, with particular attention to weapons and engineering equipment. Dabs of red lead paint, seagull droppings, and weather-worn gray paint made these ships look far older than they were. Of course, various parts were "midnight requisitioned" by enterprising crewmen aboard active sister ships. After eight years of being in reserve, most of the flush deck destroyers that remained looked pretty sorry. However, in September 1929, it was decided that 48 active wartime-built destroyers would be replaced by a similar number from the inactive fleet sites in San Diego and Philadelphia.

The possibility of prying funds from the U.S. Congress for new destroyer construction was so remote as to not be considered. Precious naval dollars were being used to rebuild existing capital ships and 8-inch-gun heavy cruisers up to the 10,000-ton limit allowed by the treaties. Besides, inactive fleet anchorage were bulging with practically brand-new destroyers. Maintaining a huge fleet of surplus ships had the negative effect of preventing money from being allocated for modern replacements. As a consequence, the Navy embarked on a rather ambitious plan to use what little funding was available to trade in a poorly performing vessel for one with a few miles under her keel.

Of the 72 "tin cans" in active service, 48 would each be tethered to a replacement, and as quickly as possible, the ugly ducklings from "red lead row" would take their place in the fleet. The formerly spic-and-span units would then be sent to the scrap yard—with the double benefit of freeing up allowable tonnage under the treaties for new construction.

In the Philadelphia Navy Yard, 14 destroyers were selected from the 85 in residence, and in San Diego, 34 were culled out for new life. It was important

Workmen repair and clean up a flush decker at the Brooklyn Navy Yard for transfer to Great Britain under the 1940 "destroyers for bases" deal. Great Britain was desperate for any warships that could help fend off the U-boat campaign that had nearly brought the country to its knees. Anchor chains litter the foredeck of the destroyer, and a sailor works on the forward 4-inch/.50-caliber deck gun. *Treasure Island Museum–SFCB*

to spend an adequate amount of time on this process, but not endanger the nation by having a large percentage of its destroyers under repair. The 34 ships withdrawn from the Pacific Fleet left only two destroyers available—the USS *Decatur* (DD-341) and the USS *Litchfield* (DD-336).

In the San Diego harbor, the ships were paired off—a red lead row survivor and the destroyer selected for replacement. With the help of yard tenders such as the USS *Medusa*, USS *Melville*, and the light cruiser USS *Omaha* (CL-4), crews of the old ships assisted by yard specialists began to build a new ship out of two. For curious onlookers it must have seemed strange to watch the progressive destruction of what began as a brand-new looking ship and the transformation of an ugly duckling into a new fleet unit. A few destroyers were towed to the Mare Island Naval Shipyard, where they were repaired near the tidal flats, and in Philadelphia, the work was done in the reserve fleet basin.

The crews soon discovered that those ships that were in the best shape had been well taken care of before being decommissioned. The machinery had been thoroughly cleaned and greased. More common defects included defective condensers, worn bearings, and reduction gears out of alignment. Also, those areas where water had been allowed to stand had caused severe rust damage and bulkhead leaks. Wiring had not fared well during the long lay-up, and the hulls had sea growth on them that was thicker than most old boatswains' mates had ever seen. Wooden bearings (lignum vitae) used in the strut bearings were in some instances damaged by marine growth and required replacement, but overall, the old ships were in remarkably good condition.

All of the 48 ships needed to be updated with modern electronics, and it was not unusual to see lighters loaded with piles of junk (up to and including entire bridge structures) taken from the ships for disposal. Fire control and torpedo-tube wiring was usually replaced in all of the ships that were brought out of storage. By June 1930, the last of the renovated ships were ready to take their place in the fleet, complete with their crews who were thoroughly familiar with the new ships. The 48 destroyers, which five months before looked factory fresh, were now stripped down and worn looking. On the West Coast, the 34 ships were taken to the Mare Island Navy Yard, where they were decommissioned and sold for scrap. The remaining ships of Destroyer Squadron Eleven, seven of which had run aground in 1923, were disposed of through sale or scrapping at the yard. Commercial shipbreakers bought some of the hulks for as little as $200, and the USS *Moody*

The battleship USS *California* (BB-44) is alongside a fitting out pier at the Mare Island Navy Yard in this image taken on April 1, 1921. In the background near the causeway, a number of flush deck destroyers that are on inactive status can be seen. Precious naval funding was spent first on the development and maintenance of the battleship, and what was left of the budget went to "experimental items" such as naval aviation, submarines, and antisubmarine warfare. It would be 20 years after this photograph was taken before the fallacy of the battleship mindset was exposed and an emergency building priority was set on destroyers and destroyer-type vessels. The battleship was of little value against carrier launched aircraft or Japanese and German fleet submarines. *U.S. Navy*

(DD-277) gained a modicum of fame when she was used as a target ship in the MGM film *Sea Pigs*.

One of the replacement destroyers, the USS *Zane* (DD-337), was later converted to a destroyer minesweeper (DMS-14) for World War II service. It served as rough background material for one of its officers, Herman Wouk, who wrote the most famous novel of navy life at sea to come out of World War II, *The Caine Mutiny* (1951, Doubleday & Co.).

Other ships brought out of "red lead row" in 1930 included the USS *Greer*(DD-145), which made the first attack on a German U-boat on September 4, 1941, three months before war was declared. The U-boat fired first with a torpedo, and the *Greer* responded with a depth charge attack. Another torpedo was fired, and it, too, missed. The *Greer* alternatively listened and attacked, but the U-boat escaped after suffering some very rough treatment.

The USS *Jacob Jones* (DD-130) was another of the 34 flush deckers brought out of San Diego's red lead row; however, she did not fare as well as some of her fellow destroyers. On February 28, 1942, while on patrol off the Delaware Capes, the destroyer was hit by two or three torpedoes fired by the *U-578*. She quickly broke up and sank, leaving only 11 survivors to be rescued by *Eagle Boat #56*.

While it seemed that most inactive fleet sites were crowded mainly with destroyers and other escort and patrol vessels, as the years wore on and the beginning of World War II drew closer, other ships found their way into reserve sites. Older submarines, cargo vessels, and ships destined to become historic reminders of past victories (such as the USS *Olympia* at the Philadelphia Navy Yard) were placed in storage.

The starboard 4-inch/50 caliber gun mount and its youthful crew aboard the USS *Ward* (DD-139). This gun shot a hole through the conning tower of a Japanese midget submarine that attempted to penetrate Pearl Harbor in the early morning of December 7, 1941. The *Ward* then dropped depth charges that finished the job and sent the intruder to the bottom. The *Ward* had just come out of red lead row at the San Diego Destroyer Base and quickly became its most famous alumna. *Treasure Island Museum–SFCB*

In July 1940, the United States offered 50 destroyers of the "red lead fleet" to Great Britain in exchange for 99-year leases on selected bases from Newfoundland to Trinidad. The deal was by no means equitable. The destroyers were now in bad condition, but were desperately needed by the Royal Navy and Royal Canadian Navy for antisubmarine patrol and convoy escort duty. Complaints about leaky bulkheads and poor seakeeping were just words. The ships proved to be a godsend to a nation nearing the end of her proverbial rope.

The demands of a war that the United States was becoming a part of required that other vessels were recalled for service if they had any possible life left. Destroyers that had rested for nearly 20 years were brought out and refitted for mine-laying, minesweeping, and aircraft tenders. One of these was the USS *Ward* (DD-139), which had experienced temporary notoriety when she was built in a record-setting 17 days by the Mare Island Navy Yard. She had been decommissioned on June 21, 1921, and recommissioned on February 13, 1941. For 20 years she sat in "red lead row" at the San Diego Destroyer Base. During those two decades—and especially during the latter years—she was reduced to a carcass that only upon close inspection resembled a destroyer. As ships were being recommissioned at an accelerating rate, the *Ward* (last in line) was the likely target for parts, hunters and outright thieves. By the time it was the *Ward*'s turn to come out of reserve, it was necessary to rebuild or replace most of her machinery. She emerged from the repair base a nearly new but wholly obsolete destroyer. The U.S. Navy had built 100 new destroyers, 18 heavy cruisers, 19 light cruisers, 6 battleships (4 World War I design), and 7 fleet aircraft carriers during the time the *Ward* had rusted and waited. Yet, on December 7, 1941, it was the *Ward* that fired the first shot of the Pacific War. With depth charges and gunfire, the red lead fleet tin can sank an attacking Japanese midget submarine at the entrance to Pearl Harbor.

With the growing war fever, the U.S. Navy began to expand in all ship classes, and added to the continuous withdrawal of serviceable ships from the inactive sites. The number of the ships in red lead row quickly dwindled, and by the eve of war in December 1941, few decommissioned ships were left. The Japanese attack on Pearl Harbor effectively put a temporary end to the "red lead fleet" period in U.S. Naval history. Anything and everything that could float or be made to float was to be needed in the next world war.

The indomitable Liberty ship. Shown are nine of the cargo ships being outfitted for service. Next they will take on a crew, load cargo, and do what they were designed for— make a transportation bridge from the United States to Europe. Hundreds would return to be laid up for future emergencies after World War II. Treasure Island Museum—SFCB

Chapter Six

WORLD WAR II

THE SEEDS OF WAR: 1941–1945

International observers, including the U.S. Navy, became uncomfortable with the potential competition posed by Japan in the Pacific. This was brought to the forefront after the defeat of the Czar's Navy at the Battle of Tsushima in 1905 during the Russo-Japanese War. Fifty years after being opened up to Western ways, Japan was now an international player. In 1905 the Russo-Japanese War was settled by the signing of the Treaty of Portsmouth with President Theodore Roosevelt as its catalyst. He was awarded the Nobel Peace Prize for his efforts.

This shows the might of the U.S. Navy on maneuvers off the southern California coast on October 10, 1939, scarcely a month after war broke out in Europe. The battleship USS *Mississippi* (BB-41) turns to follow another *New Mexico*-class battleship in one of the periodic demonstrations of raw sea power for the benefit of the Japanese. *Treasure Island Museum–SFCB*

By 1905, the Japanese had become intensely nationalist and historically imperialistic. Many of their senior military and government leaders were unhappy with the terms of the Treaty of Portsmouth and harbored ill will toward President Roosevelt for allowing Russia to escape from paying a huge indemnity for the war. This began an open wariness of both nations about their future intentions in the Pacific.

No longer were the U.S. Navy and the Congress singularly concentrating on the status of European naval expansion programs. In addition to the growth of the German navy, the U.S. Navy had a potential contender in the Pacific. It was not all one-sided,

however, because the Japanese now saw the United States in the same way. Added to the problem of Japanese naval growth were incidents in the United States that began to further alienate the Japanese. The Japanese felt the United States was prejudiced against them as a race, and this was foundational to their relationship with the American people at all levels. It was manifested in various immigration policies and Hollywood films that usually stereotyped the Japanese in a negative if not comical way. There was some truth to the way the Japanese perceived how they were regarded by the United States. Unfortunately, this stereotype that was so well known in the United States did not fit the actual image of the determined Japanese soldier on the battlefield. Nor did American military beliefs that Japanese weapons were poorly designed prove true as so many Allied warships discovered when struck by the ship-killing "long lance" torpedo.

In 1906, the San Francisco Board of Education decided to segregate Asian children from Caucasian students, and this caused an international incident. In that same year, Japanese sealers began poaching in the Aleutians, which aggravated an already tense domestic situation. The capital ships of the U.S. Fleet were ordered back to their U.S. home ports in case of war with Japan. The poaching issue was quickly settled, and the City of San Francisco relented on its segregationist policy. Japan resolved to restrict emigration to the United States by a gentlemen's agreement with the U.S. government. This was a temporary solution to a problem that would become larger and more dangerous over the next three decades.

The Japanese grew in stature and strength up through World War I and were able to secure island bases from the defeated Germans. Unlike the British and French, the Japanese had emerged from World War I unscathed and in satisfactory economic health—much like the United States. However, it was obvious to most diplomats that some mechanism was necessary to restrict the continued proliferation of naval weapons, and in particular the capital ship. Some form of agreement was welcomed by the economically devastated European powers, and the United States and Great Britain were anxious to put Japan in its proper place in the world naval community.

In 1922, the Naval Armament Treaty signed in Washington, D.C., allowed Japan 315,000 tons, or 60 percent, of the United States' and Great Britain's 525,000 total combatant tonnage. The treaty also

Flush deck destroyers USS *Rueben James* (DD-245) and USS *Truxton* (DD-229) sit outside New York Harbor on September 7, 1940. The *Rueben James* went into mothballs on January 20, 1931, and was back on duty on March 9, 1932. She was torpedoed by a German U-boat on October 31, 1941, five weeks before the attack on Pearl Harbor. The *Truxton*, one of the few World War I destroyers that avoided a boneyard, was lost due to grounding on February 18, 1942. The *Truxton* lost 110 crew members as the old destroyer broke up on the coast of Newfoundland. *Treasure Island Museum–SFCB*

provided for a status quo in Pacific-area fortifications and naval base maintenance with the condition, "This restriction does not preclude such repair or replacement of worn-out weapons and equipment as is customary in naval and military establishments in time of peace." Also agreed upon was the provision that ships reaching a certain age (generally 20-plus years) would be scrapped. Those specified were the battleships IJN *Kongo, Kirishima, Fuso, Ise,* and *Nagato,* as well as American battleships USS *Nevada, New Mexico, California,* and *Oklahoma.* All of the ships would fight two decades later in World War II. Although the Japanese agreed to the treaty, their government felt slighted to be considered only 60 percent as good as Great Britain and the United States. They immediately set out to build ships in violation of the 1922 treaty and the agreements that were laid out in 1930. They formally abandoned the treaty

process in 1936 and continued building ships, but no longer with such secrecy. They also fortified their Pacific island holdings, including the Gilbert and Mariana Islands, and prepared for a probable war with the United States and Great Britain.

The U.S. Navy was not simply sitting back and observing Japanese maneuvers in the Pacific. Soon after the signing of the Washington Naval Treaty, the U.S. Navy decided to take most of the battle fleet from the West Coast to the South Seas, New Zealand, and Australia. On March 2, 1925, a line of battleships including the *Nevada, New Mexico,* and *Oklahoma* cruisers and destroyers, in a line miles in length, sailed from southern California to Pearl Harbor and the South Seas, and returned to San Pedro on September 26, 1925. The 16,000-mile journey of the U.S. Fleet without its having to reprovision or refuel more than few times had two

The battleship USS *Nevada* (BB-36) ran aground at Hospital Point in Pearl Harbor on December 8, 1941, the day after the Japanese air attack. The small harbor tug, USS *Hoga* (YT-146/YTM-146) can be seen off the port bow of the burning ship. The tug fought fires on the stranded ship and went to the assistance of damaged ships all over the harbor during and after the attack. *TIM–SFCB*

purposes: the cruise proved that American naval might could defend our allies down under, and operate as far as Japanese home waters in fighting condition. The mistake made by the Czarist Navy in the 1905 Battle of Tsushima would not be repeated by the U.S. Navy if the time came for aggressive action. The Japanese press made much of this cruise as threatening to international relations, and began to step up its campaign of anti-Western hatred.

The Japanese had designs on China, and throughout the late 1920s and up to the beginning of the Pacific War in 1941, Japan progressively attacked and captured more Chinese territory. Protests were lodged and in April 1932, the U.S. Navy made another demonstration on the West Coast that was designed to put the brakes on Japanese ambition. More than 120 U.S. warships sailed up and down the California coast. This array of American naval power impressed both the Japanese and more than 250,000 people who watched from the beaches. Unfortunately, it was somewhat of a hollow parade. The ships were in a

poor state of upkeep, and the fleet was 30,000 sailors short of minimum steaming needs. The country was in the throes of economic chaos, but it was still vital to put the best foot forward.

In the years that led up to World War II, Japan continued with a campaign of ruthless conquests in China and secretly built a modern fleet of battleships, fleet aircraft carriers, fast cruisers, and destroyers. The Imperial Japanese Navy also committed resources to night-fighting optics and tactics, torpedoes (long lance), fighter aircraft (Zero), and torpedo bombers (Kate).

Imperial Japan was not the only enemy of the United States in the coming war. In 1933, Germany was fully overtaken by Adolf Hitler, and the spread of Nazism was inevitable. With it came nationalism on a scale unprecedented in human history. It took the form of murdering millions of innocent men, women, and children, and seeking revenge for the destruction wrought on Germany from the World War I Treaty of Versailles. Germany began rearming as soon as it became obvious that no country was going to object with military intervention.

The German Navy capitalized on its former successes in World War I by concentrating much of its energy on building U-boats and heavily armed surface raiders (*Graf Spee* pocket battleship and the *Bismarck* battleship classes). By the summer of 1939, the German Navy was not nearly ready for a major war, but Hitler was anxious to begin. On September 1, 1939, the German army and Luftwaffe (air force) attacked Poland. On September 3rd, France and Great Britain reluctantly declared war on Nazi Germany, and the most devastating event in the twentieth century had begun. During the uneasy 26 months between the start of the war and the official entry of the United States was a historical period known as "short of war." It became increasingly obvious that the United States would support the Allied cause against what was to become the Axis powers of Germany, Japan, and Italy.

On September 5, 1939, President Franklin Roosevelt declared that the United States was neutral in this conflict; however, the U.S. Navy would guarantee the safety of ships in U.S. waters. Fortunately, the Navy had been augmented with a number of modern vessels including more than 100 destroyers, 9 *Brooklyn-St Louis*-class light cruisers, submarines, and aircraft carriers. In addition to the USS *Saratoga* (CV-3) and USS *Lexington* (CV-2), the Navy had commissioned fleet carriers USS *Ranger* (CV-4), USS *Yorktown* (CV-5), and USS *Enterprise* (CV-6). This had all stemmed from $238 million in funding that had been set aside by President Roosevelt for a 32-vessel naval rebuilding program that was beginning in mid-1933.

The Navy still needed more ships to sustain a dedicated two-ocean navy,

and on June 17, 1940, three days after the fall of France, $4 billion more was granted for additional ships. Before new ships could be built, the events of time would not wait. As a temporary expedient, much of the red lead fleet was recommissioned and returned to active service. By December 1941, there were few ships left in reserve.

As the United States slid closer and closer to the brink of war, its Navy was the first to feel the sting of battle. In December 1937 the gunboat USS *Panay* (PR-5) was sunk in the Yangtze River by Japanese land-based bombers, even though the well-known American gunboat was unmistakably identified with U.S. flags. Two men were killed and 43 were wounded in the unprovoked attack. The U.S. Navy was active in a declared war zone protecting American lives and interests, and the same kind of incident was to happen again and again as the war loomed in the future.

On the other side of the world, on April 10, 1941, the destroyer USS *Niblack* (DD-424) depth charged a

The old harbor tug USS *Hoga* is sandwiched in between two other tugs at the Suisun Bay Reserve Fleet anchorage on October 18, 1999. The tug served the Navy until 1962, when it was transferred to the Oakland Fire Department. She was finally retired in 1995 and now awaits some disposition. The still seaworthy little craft is the last surviving U.S. Navy vessel that was present during the Japanese attack on Pearl Harbor on December 7, 1941. *Author's collection*

German U-boat that sank a Dutch freighter. The USS *Greer* (DD-145) was unsuccessfully attacked with torpedoes from the German U-boat *U-652* on September 4, 1941. So far in the undeclared war in the Atlantic, weapons were missing, but on October 17, 1941, the destroyer USS *Kearny* (DD-432) was hit by a torpedo amidships while off the coast of Greenland. Only the strength of her construction and her determined crew saved her from being lost. Two weeks later, the destroyer USS *Reuben James* (DD-245) was not so fortunate. The old "red lead row" veteran from World War I was sunk by the German *U-562* on October 31, 1941, while escorting a convoy from Halifax, Nova Scotia. The 155-member crew was lost in the icy waters, and the *Reuben James* had the unhappy distinction of being the first U.S. Navy ship sunk by the Axis. Six weeks later, the war began in earnest for the United States with the attack on air, army, and naval installations in and around Pearl Harbor on the morning of December 7, 1941.

World War II

The Navy Department was well aware of the probability of war with Japan, Italy, and Germany—signatories to the Tripartite Pact agreed upon on September 27, 1940. This pact guaranteed a unit-

The USS *Hornet* (CV-8) launches a B-25 bomber from its pitching deck on April 18, 1942. The first bomber to attack the Japanese mainland was piloted by Lt. Col. Jimmy Doolittle. The USS *Enterprise* (CV-6) provided air cover for the task force because the deck of the *Hornet* was crowded with Army aircraft. *Author's collection*

ed front against the Allies. The U.S. Navy was ill prepared for a multi-ocean war and on the eve of the Pearl Harbor attack, the Navy had the following assets in its warship inventory:

Battleships: 15 modernized yet obsolete World War I–era battleships; 2 modern, fast 16-inch-gun-armed battleships (*Washington* [BB-56]/*North Carolina* [BB-55]) in commission; 4 fast 16-inch-gun-armed *South Dakota*-class under construction; and 4 fast 16-inch-gun-armed *Iowa*-class in the early stages of construction.

Aircraft Carriers: 7 fleet carriers plus 3 *Essex*-class fast carriers already laid down with 23 planned to follow; 9 *Independence*-class (CVL) light carriers; and scores of escort carriers (CVE).

Cruisers (heavy/light/antiaircraft): 18 heavy cruisers, 19 light cruisers, and 6 antiaircraft cruisers.

Destroyers: 171 vessels, of which 72 dated to World War I, and 27 were early-1930s designs barely suitable for the rigors of continuous South Pacific or North Atlantic combat. The remaining 72 were satisfactory and led the way for hundreds more to be built during the war, including more than 300 destroyer escort-type ships.

Submarines: 114 active boats with some dating back to 1918; however, 79 modern *Gato*-class boats were under development.

Fleet Train/Auxiliaries/Amphibious Warfare: more than 250 mine craft and a growing number of landing craft. This was a fraction of what would be required.

Sea forces afloat were arrayed into three major fleets: Atlantic, Pacific, and Asiatic. The Atlantic Fleet was to guard the American East Coast and coastal areas in the Caribbean in the event of war with the Axis. The Pacific Fleet's primary duty in the event of war with Japan was to protect the American West Coast and its outer defenses, including the Territory of Hawaii. With this accomplished, the battle force would steam to the aid of the Asiatic Fleet, which was tasked to fight a delaying action. It was established in War Department planning that the Japanese would move to occupy the Philippines as a steppingstone in their overall plan of conquest. It would be imprudent to allow a

The port side of the heavy cruiser USS *San Francisco* (CA-38) is shown after fighting the Naval Battle of Guadalcanal on November 12 and 13, 1942. The badly damaged cruiser was being repaired at the Mare Island Naval Shipyard. The *San Francisco* survived the war and entered the Atlantic Reserve Fleet (Philadelphia Group) in February 1946. She remained there until she was sold on September 9, 1959. *U.S. Navy*

large enemy army in the midst of their line of communication and supply; consequently, the Asiatic Fleet and other U.S. and Philippine armed forces would have to be neutralized.

The Asiatic Fleet was an outgrowth of Admiral Dewey's Far Eastern squadron and had evolved to become a token collection of older vessels bolstered with 29 submarines. Its flagship was the heavy cruiser USS *Houston* (CA-30), which had just relieved the USS *Augusta* (CA-31) on November 22, 1940. The *Houston* had just finished an overhaul and was armed with new 1.1-inch antiaircraft weapons. In the event of war with Japan, it was assumed (on paper) that both navies would meet at sea—a remarkably similar strategy to that of the Russian Navy in 1905—with a clash of two battle lines and the winner take all. An all-encompassing attack from the air was not envisioned when the U.S. plan was developed, nor was the value of the aircraft carrier properly assessed.

The Japanese Imperial General Staff had been planning such a raid for months, which would put the U.S. Fleet out of action and allow for unhampered Japanese expansion and the capture of vital oil,

rubber, and other resources in the Dutch East Indies and the Malay Peninsula. Air and naval attacks were coordinated and scheduled for a large number of critical Allied strongholds. It began with Pearl Harbor.

The Japanese planes began to attack shortly before 8 A.M. It was presupposed that a coordinated air attack on American air bases and major fleet units on a Sunday morning would meet with the least resistance. The planning was correct, and although the U.S. response was spirited, it was insufficient to prevent the huge losses that occurred. There was a combined total of 361 aircraft launched from six fleet carriers. The raid was divided into two attacks, but the targets were obvious: aircraft carriers, battleships, cruisers, patrol planes, and ground aircraft. Shortly after 10 A.M., the attack was over, and with a loss of only 29 aircraft, the Japanese turned and headed back to a triumphant welcome. U.S. forces on Oahu were decimated, including the loss of 2,403 service personnel; and a large percentage of bomber, fighter, and patrol aircraft. The battleships *Oklahoma, California, Arizona,* and *West Virginia* were all sunk. Other ships such as the battleships

The destroyers USS *Barry* (DD-248) and USS *Borie* (DD-215) were photographed from the escort carrier USS *Card* (CVE-11) on November 2, 1943, in the Atlantic. The night before, the *Borie* fought a duel with the *U-405*, which climaxed when the old destroyer rammed her opponent. Both crews fought it out with any and all weapons at hand. The *Borie* (low in the water, right) won, but sank shortly after being photographed due to severe bow damage. The *Barry* was an alumni of a warship boneyard. *Treasure Island Museum—SFCB*

Nevada, Tennessee, Maryland, and *Pennsylvania* were damaged but easily salvageable. Fortunately, the damage to the shipyard, submarine base, and fleet oil reserves was minimal. Luckily, the carriers were not in port or there would have been a vastly different outcome in the Pacific War.

Within days, the United States was at war with all Axis powers and over the next six months, the United States suffered one tactical defeat after another. Guam, Wake Island, the Philippines, Singapore, and the resource-rich Netherlands East Indies fell to the Japanese octopus-like attack. The U.S. Asiatic Fleet, led by the venerable heavy cruiser USS *Houston* (CA-30) with 13 flush deck destroyers and the *Omaha*-class light cruiser USS *Marblehead* (CL-12), fought a delaying action against overwhelming Japanese naval and air units that ended in near annihilation by March 1, 1942. The *Houston*, most of the flush deck destroyers, and the U.S. Navy's first aircraft carrier, the USS *Langley* (CV-1/AV-3), fell victim to Japanese air attack or surface ships. The Asiatic Fleet was destroyed.

At the same time that the Japanese seemed to be victorious at every turn, the German U-boat menace was such that its submarines attacked American shipping within the shine of night lights of American cities on the East Coast. Some of the German submariners referred to the slaughter of ships at sea in the early days as the "happy time." Before the United States and Great Britain mobilized their antisubmarine program, many U-boats were sinking an average of eight ships per patrol. The U.S. Navy armed anything and everything that would float including sailboats and private yachts to patrol the coastline pending the explosion in escort-ship building in shipyards all over the United States.

All of the military reverses the Allies were suffering in Southeast Asia, Russia, North Africa, and the Mediterranean in early 1942 seemed to confirm the propaganda that the Axis powers were invincible. In fact, the Japanese were so confident of their future success that many officers spoke of the "victory illness" that can make an armed force too sure of itself. It was so pervasive that after Japanese aircraft carrier pilots learned that Midway Island was to be attacked in June 1942, many asked that their future mail be forwarded there.

The Allied cause needed a shot in the arm, and it came in the form of the Halsey-Doolittle raid. Army Air Corps Lt. Col. James "Jimmy" Doolittle secretly trained pilots and crews to fly 16 twin-engine *B-25 Mitchell* bombers from the deck of a fleet carrier. On April 18, 1942, Task Force 16, composed of carriers USS *Enterprise* (CV-6) and USS *Hornet* (CV-8) and their escorts, steamed toward the intended launch point 500 miles from Tokyo. The force encountered a Japanese picket boat that was on patrol nearly 700 miles from Tokyo. Cruisers USS *Salt Lake City,* USS *Vincennes* (CA-44), and USS *Nashville* (CL-43) responded, and the *Nashville* smothered the boat with 6-inch gunfire. Adm. William Halsey and Col. Doolittle decided to launch the bombers that were on the deck of the *Hornet.* The margin of safety was extreme, but concern about the warning potentially sent by the picket boat overruled caution. At a distance of 668 miles from Tokyo, Doolittle launched beginning at 7:25 A.M. All 16 bombers successfully left the deck of the pitching carrier and bombed various Japanese home island targets. The raid itself did little damage, however the boost in public morale was felt from San Francisco to London.

The war in the Pacific heated up after the raid with the Coral Sea Battle fought over May 7 and 8, 1942, where the United States lost the carrier USS *Lexington* (CV-2), fleet tanker USS *Neosho* (AO-23), and destroyer USS *Sims* (DD-409). This exchange between two distant battle groups with aircraft carriers at their hub portended a future where naval battles would be fought without ships being in sight of one another. The next opportunity for decisive combat came less than one month later with a showdown between the U.S. Navy and the Imperial Japanese Navy at the June 2–6, 1942, Battle of Midway. Admiral Isoroku Yamamoto of the Imperial Japanese Navy committed most of the Combined Fleet to bring out all remaining American naval forces for the final destruction of the U.S. carriers.

Admiral Chester Nimitz responded to what his code breakers told him about the upcoming attack and sent carriers *Enterprise, Hornet,* and *Yorktown* (CV-5) with a cruiser and destroyer escort to a point where they could intercept the Japanese. The U.S. Navy's code-breaking team had sufficiently deciphered the Japanese naval code (JN-25) to determine the Japanese target— Midway. In an air battle between both forces, the U.S. Navy lost the carrier *Yorktown* and destroyer USS *Hammann* (DD-412). The Japanese lost four fleet carriers, the *Akagi, Hiryu, Kaga,* and *Soryu.* They also lost the cream of their best pilots and hundreds of aircraft. In just minutes, American aviators blunted the sword point of Japanese naval power in the Pacific.

In the months that followed, the U.S. Navy supported the landings in the Solomon Islands and began a

series of battles fought that can only be described as street fighting at sea. Brutal, violent night engagements between Japanese, U.S., and Australian battleships, cruisers, and destroyers left sinking ships each morning. The objective of the Japanese was to eject the Marines from Guadalcanal, while the United States and its allies were determined to remain. To evacuate meant disaster and a breach in the line of communication and supply in the South Pacific. The U.S. Navy lost cruisers *Vincennes, Astoria* (CA-34), *Quincy* (CA-39), *Atlanta* (CL51), *Juneau* (CL-52), *Chicago* (CA-29), *Northampton* (CA-27), and *Helena* (CL-50) in addition to numerous destroyers, fast transports, and the carriers *Wasp* (CV-7) and *Hornet* (CV-8). The Japanese were finally stopped in early 1943, and U.S. and Allied forces began moving across the central and south Pacific to push into the inner ring of Japan's home defenses. New carriers (*Essex* and *Independence* classes), cruisers (*Cleveland* and *Baltimore* classes), destroyers (*Fletcher, Gearing,* and *Sumner* classes), destroyer escorts, amphibious ships,

In this January 8, 1945, photograph, the power of the wartime American navy can be seen at anchor. There are at least seven fast carriers in view complemented by two *Iowa*-class and one *South Dakota*-class battleships. Within two years, most of these vessels would be in a Reserve Fleet group. *TIM–SFCB*

and vessels of every possible use were coming quickly from U.S. shipyards to replace the prewar ships that were being lost. The U.S. submarine force, taking a page from U-boat tactics, helped to bring down the Japanese Empire. By the end of the war, U.S. submarines sank 276 Japanese naval vessels, including 4 carriers and 1 battleship. They also sank 8.8 million tons of Japanese merchant shipping and virtually stranded much of Japan's armed forces far from the home islands. In the summer of 1945, so many enemy ships had been sunk that targets had become scarce.

On the other side of the world, the North African landings had taken place (Operation Torch) over November 8 to 10, 1942, and Allied planners

The USS *Ward* (APD-16/DD-139) lies smoking after having been hit by a Kamikaze on December 7, 1944—three years from the date she fired the first shot of the Pacific War outside Pearl Harbor. The veteran ship was sunk by gunfire from the destroyer USS *O'Brien* (DD-725) to prevent her from becoming a menace to navigation. The captain of the *O'Brien* was none other than Commander William Outerbridge, coincidentally the captain of the *Ward* three years earlier. *Author's collection*

were gearing up for amphibious assaults on Italy and France to retake Europe from the Nazis. Before the Allies could set foot on French soil, enough men and materials were needed for a full-scale invasion. This meant that ships had to bring these assets from the United States and Canada to Great Britain and the Soviet Union. The U-boat problem had to be solved to enable safe passage. From the early days of the war, the United States and its allies systematically developed the convoy system, and by the end of 1942, the Germans began to feel the results of Allied technological work on better methods of submarine detection underwater and on the surface. In concert with these new methods and electronic aids, improvements were made in explosives (depth charges, hedgehogs), but the best solution was providing a sufficient number of well-armed escort vessels. By the end of the war, American shipyards had turned out 349 new destroyers and 420 smaller escort vessels, including the *Buckley*, *John C Butler*, and *Evarts* classes.

On June 6, 1944, otherwise known as D-Day, the invasion of Europe began with a combined total of

2,707 Allied ships in support of 66,000 troops that hit the beaches at Normandy. For the next 11 months, the Allied armies marched steadily toward Berlin from France and the Soviet Union. Both of these drives were supported by millions of tons of supplies and equipment brought by thousands of ships making one journey after another from the United States.

In the Pacific, the Allies were closing in on the Japanese home islands from the island-hopping campaigns in the central and south Pacific areas. By mid-1945, the U.S. Navy had amassed a huge number of carriers, battleships, cruisers, and destroyers. They had survived the bloody battles in the Philippine Sea (June 19–20, 1944), Leyte Gulf (October 24–25, 1944), and faced the Japanese at the invasion of Okinawa in April 1945. Here the U.S. Navy met its most formidable challenge since 1942. The Special Attack Corps, or kamikazes, was a group of aircraft piloted by men bent on suicide, and their targets were enemy ships (primarily aircraft carriers and transports) off the coast of Okinawa. These aircraft crashed into American and Allied warships and were

This is a typical postwar decommissioning ceremony aboard a major combatant. Here the prewar-built battleship USS *California* (BB-44) enters the Philadelphia Group of the Atlantic Reserve Fleet on August 10, 1946. Smaller ships had ceremonies on a greatly reduced scale. Typically, the commission pennant was hauled down and a few words said as sailors waited to get back to civilian life. *TIM–SFCB*

in essence guided missiles. They did horrific damage to 368 ships, including the carriers USS *Enterprise* (CV-6), USS *Bunker Hill* (CV-17), and USS *Intrepid* (CV-11). Thirty-two ships were sunk by this fantastic last-ditch-stand weapon, including a large number of destroyer-type ships serving on the "picket line" (radar intercept sentries posted closer to Japanese territory than the main body of the fleet). At one point, the life expectancy of a destroyer stationed on the picket line was 90 minutes or less when swarm attacks of kamikazes bore in.

The war ended before the planned Allied invasion of the Japanese home islands. Twin atomic weapons dropped on the cities of Hiroshima and Nagasaki in August 1945, aggravated by the roving attacks of U.S. submarines and naval and air force aircraft, convinced the Japanese emperor to initiate an unconditional surrender. On September 2, 1945, the Japanese government surrendered to the Allies with the signing of the instrument of surrender aboard the battleship USS *Missouri* (BB-63).

The War Ends and So Does the Need for a Huge Navy

When the war began for the United States on December 7, 1941, it was not a complete surprise to U.S. military planners, and ships by the thousands began to take shape in most naval shipyards and many private yards with access to the sea. One of the most prolific of cargo ships built to replace sunken tonnage was the venerable "ugly duckling," or 14,242-ton full-load *Liberty* ship, and later the *Victory* (15,200 tons full load) was built. By mid-1942, ships of all types were being built in assembly line style to replace shipping that was being steadily sunk by German U-boats. In 1941, the total was 4,693,000 tons, and it nearly doubled to 8,333,000 tons lost in 1942. It was critical that a bridge of ships be maintained to build up supplies and equipment in Great Britain and the Soviet Union for the eventual retaking of Europe. To this end, 275 *Victory* ships and 2,710 *Liberty* ships were built. Of these, hundreds were provided to the Soviet Union, Great Britain, and other nations opposing fascism. In addition to merchant hulls, the United States lent 1,622 naval vessels to Allied nations, including 38 escort carriers (CVE), 113 landing ship tanks (LST), and 78 destroyer escorts (DE) to Great Britain. The Soviet Union was lent 34 minesweepers (AM), 28 patrol gunboats and frigates (PC and PG), as well as 205 torpedo boats (PT). After the war, the Soviet Union returned few of the ships that were lent, falsely claiming that other nations also retained vessels in violation of lend-lease arrangements.

Aircraft assembly plants appeared all over the United States, and the 50,000 planes per year promised by President Roosevelt was achieved with a total of 296,601 aircraft. There were 86,388 tanks as well as thousands of half-tracks, jeeps, rifles, and other weapons sent worldwide bearing a "made in the USA" stamp. The United States was truly the arsenal of democracy, and these were not hollow words, as evidenced by the outpouring of goods and equipment.

Fighting the war required personnel on a scale unprecedented in U.S. history. The country had slightly less than 150,000,000 citizens at the outbreak of war, and in December 1941, there were 486,226 men and women in the sea services. The majority (383,150), were in the U.S. Navy, followed by 75,346 in the Marine Corps, and 27,730 in the Coast Guard. By the end of the war, the total number of people enlisted in the military had increased almost tenfold to 4,064,455. There were 3,408,347 men and women in the Navy, 485,833 in the USMC, and 170,275 in the Coast Guard. Overall, the United States trained 15 million service personnel who served in the armed forces.

By the end of the war, shipyards in the United States had produced 5,400 cargo ships of all types, 64,500 landing craft, and 6,500 naval vessels with an aggregate total of 28,000,000 gross tons.

This is a mass grave for nine U.S. destroyers in one of the Philadelphia Naval Shipyard's drydocks. Five of the "tin cans" being scrapped are old flush deckers including the USS *Whipple* (DD-217) and the USS *Stringham* (DD-83). The other four were *Porter*-class destroyer leaders built in the 1930s, shown in this March 14, 1946, image. *Author's collection*

The day the war ended, the U.S. Navy had vessels in almost every part of the world. The fleet contained 40 fleet carriers with more under construction, 24 battleships, 36 heavy cruisers, 57 light cruisers, and 450 destroyers. In addition, there were 79 escort carriers, 263 submarines, and 359 destroyer escorts. There were hundreds of minesweepers, patrol boats, amphibious craft of all types, and a massive fleet service force of tenders, repair ships, and medical evacuee ships. In short, the largest navy in the world or that the world had ever seen, was now temporarily unemployed.

Most of the 4 million men and women in the sea services wanted to return to civilian life, and even before the Japanese surrendered, a crude method of discharging service personnel had been developed. When the war ended, civilian sailors clamored to return to the United States. On one patrol craft in the South Pacific, all but one officer had sufficient "points" for immediate discharge. He had no skills as a navigator, and an old chief (CPO) simply told the young officer to weigh anchor and steam eastward—they were bound to run into North America if the fuel and food held out!

Before any ships could be returned to the United States for decommissioning, it was imperative that former prisoners of war and the sick and wounded be returned. To this end, as many ships as could be outfitted were pressed into service to return American service personnel back home. Carriers such as the *Enterprise, Monterrey* (CVL-26), *Bataan* (CVL-29), *Cape Gloucester* (CVE-109), and battleships *New Mexico* (BB-40), *Idaho* (BB-42), and *North Carolina* (BB-55) brought back thousands of men and women. Cruisers, destroyers, and other vessels, with the exception of LSTs, were used to bring back our troops. The flat-bottomed LSTs were used to return thousands of Japanese troops to their homeland. This entire process was dubbed *Operation Magic Carpet*, and by late October 1945, it was a worldwide phenomenon. Demobilization was stepped up in the winter of 1945/1946, and by March 1946, more than 3.1 million personnel had been returned, and of that total, 1.3 million rode ships back to the United States. Now it was time to deal with the leftover vessels.

As the price of steel went sky high, battleships and destroyers were quickly sent to the chopping block after the end of World War II. Shown are the battleships USS *Wyoming* (BB-32) (right), USS *New Mexico* (BB-40) (bottom left), and USS *Idaho* (BB-42) at the Lipsett Inc. scrapyard facility in Newark, New Jersey on December 16, 1947. *Author's collection*

The Liberty ship SS Jeremiah O'Brien is moored as part of a museum on San Francisco Bay. Of the 2,710 Liberty ships built, only the O'Brien and the SS John Brown have survived intact. The O'Brien was towed from the Suisun Bay Reserve Fleet anchorage and carefully outfitted to her 1944 appearance. She made the trip to Normandy for the 50-year anniversary of D-Day on June 6, 1994—she was the only one. Author's collection

Chapter Seven
DISPOSITION OF POSTWAR SHIPS

A NAVAL GIANT IS PUT TO SLEEP

The immensity of the post–World War II fleet of ships made the surplus at the end of the previous wars seem insignificant. Ships of all types and kinds were returning to the United States for some form of disposition. It was obvious that there was no immediate need for a large naval and service force, and consequent plans had to be made to scale down the number of vessels to the appropriate force structure needed, and decisions had to be made on those that would not remain in active status. First it was necessary to determine which ships would be retained as active or reserve, and which the navy or national defense had no further need for. Survey boards were convened to inspect vessels for their potential. The process began in earnest.

Almost immediately, 143 ships were declared unserviceable and abandoned in Buckner Bay at Okinawa. Typhoon *Louise* swept through the area over October 9 and 10, 1945, and 234 ships were grounded and/or severely damaged. Ships too badly damaged were stripped and decommissioned on the spot. Back in the United States, ships were arriving in droves and began to clog major harbors and shipyards.

A large number of vessels were sold for scrap or to private parties for pleasure or commercial use. Many of the converted yachts that were so desperately needed for ASW patrol during the early days of the war had already been returned to their former owners. The next ships to be examined were elderly service craft, cargo vessels, and warships not worthy of future preservation. In selected harbors on the U.S. coastline, ships were put up for auction and sold, but not before they were

The badly damaged hulk of the *Cleveland*-class cruiser conversion aircraft carrier USS *Independence* (CVL-22) is moored in the San Francisco Naval Shipyard. The highly radioactive ship is shown shortly after returning from being a target ship in the July 1946 Operation Crossroads atomic bomb tests in the Marshall Islands. To the left and right are two *Essex*-class aircraft carriers that had already been mothballed. The *Independence* was later sunk on January 29, 1951. *Author's collection*

formally discharged from the U.S. Navy, Coast Guard, or other federal government ownership. For old battleships like the USS *California* down to the destroyer USS *Whipple* (DD-217), a decommissioning ceremony was held. On the larger ships, a band might be present as well as an honor guard. Appropriate words were said, and national ensign and commission pennant hauled down. On the smaller ships, there was less pomp and ceremony,

In one of the many boneyards created after World War II, at least 10 destroyer-type ships, 5 land ship tanks (LST), and other miscellaneous vessels are shown anchored. This is a small part of the Hudson River basin on April 20, 1946. In other areas of this anchorage, hundreds of other ships will be stored. Freshwater basins are well suited to preserving ships for the future. *Treasure Island Museum—SFCB*

Victory ships moored in the Suisun Bay Reserve Fleet in this October 1999 photograph. Outboard is the SS *Sioux Falls Victory* moored next to eight sister ships. Few of these World War II, Korean, and Vietnam veterans still exist. *Author's collection*

This is an overhead view of the Suisun Bay Reserve Fleet anchorage at its peak after World War II. There are at least 500 vessels present. The station ship to the middle right next to the shore was the ancient mine layer USS *Oglala* (CM-4), that was built in 1917 and raised from the bottom of Pearl Harbor after she sank due to the torpedo damage to her neighbor, the cruiser USS *Helena* (CL-50) on December 7, 1941.
Suisun Bay Reserve Fleet

and the only observers to the end of a gallant vessel were uninterested shipyard workers who might pause for a moment. Ships destined for the scrap heap were herded to scrap yards sometimes in large lots or singly like the battleships *New Mexico*, *Idaho*, and *Wyoming*, which ended up in Newark, New Jersey. There, Lipsett Inc. of New York began the process of scrapping its purchases. Steel prices were high after the war and the public clamored for new automobiles, washing machines, and the comforts of home that had almost been forgotten during the war.

The first to go were the flush deck four-piper destroyers from World War I. They were demilitarized (weapons and munitions removed) and sold. Many were on the auction block before the war ended, and within two years, the flush deckers were but a memory. Coincidental to the old four-piper destroyers were the *Omaha*-class light cruisers (also four pipers). Within months of the war's end, all but one of the 10 quaint-looking cruisers of this class were slated for the scrap yard. The Soviet Union refused to return the former USS *Milwaukee* (CL-5) until 1949, and then she, too, was sold for scrap in December of that year.

Some vessels never were offered for sale to the public nor slated for preservation. These ships were to be employed for experimental use or as targets for active and reserve units. In July 1946, more than 70 vessels were exposed to two atomic blasts at Bikini Atoll in the Marshall Islands. *Operation Crossroads* was designed to test the ability of the Navy to withstand nuclear weaponry. The aircraft carriers USS *Saratoga* (CV-3) and USS Independence (CVL-22) were subjected to the blast. The *Saratoga* was lost, and the *Independence* was nearly destroyed. The U.S. Navy's oldest battleship, the USS *Arkansas* (BB-33), upended and sank; however, the *Pennsylvania*, *New York*, and *Nevada* survived to be sunk later. Many of the ships not highly exposed to the blast and radiation were returned to the San Francisco Naval Shipyard for examination and scrapping.

As to the ships that were to be laid up, there were two federal agencies that carried out what became known as "mothballing." Ships being laid up that were considered vital in an emergency—versus those that filled a lower priority of being reactivated—were identified as part of the overall plan. The highest priority for reactivation included modern aircraft carriers, battleships including the *Iowa* class, cruisers, and war/postwar-built destroyers. The amount of damage suffered during the war and the vessel's overall wear were also considered.

Noncombatant vessels were generally under the auspices of the U.S. Maritime Commission, which at the end of the war, had the largest single fleet of merchant vessels in the world. The total cost to the taxpayers beginning in 1937 had been $13 billion, and of the estimated 6,400 ships built, 5,000 vessels were still on the books as of the end of the war. This number is somewhat deceptive, as 1,200 of the vessels were small craft, and several lent to the Soviet Union never made it back. For years to come, poorly disguised *Liberty* ships flying the hammer and

The two *North Carolina*-class battleships, the USS *North Carolina* (BB-55) and USS *Washington* (BB-56), sit in reserve at one of the nation's warship boneyards at Bayonne, New Jersey. In this photograph taken on February 25, 1951, the paint is peeling and weathered. Neither of these ships will become active again. The *North Carolina* became a museum ship, and the *Washington* was sold for scrap on May 24, 1951. *TIM–SFCB*

sickle could be seen in many ports, but were rarely in the West.

The National Defense Reserve Fleet (NDRF) was created to preserve and store those vessels that were not sold for commercial use or for scrap. The Maritime Commission offered very liberal sales terms for slightly used *Liberty, Victory,* or *T-2* tankers, but by the end of the 1946 fiscal year, the fleet consisted of 1,421 ships anchored in eight sites. The number of vessels peaked in 1950 at 2,277. The sites chosen were Astoria, Oregon; Beaumont, Texas; Olympia, Washington; James River, Virginia; Suisun Bay, California; Mobile, Alabama; Hudson River, New York; and Wilmington, North Carolina. These sites were often used for warship storage as well.

The criteria for site selection boiled down to common sense. The first requirement was fresh water—or at least a location as far from saltwater as necessary to reduce organism growth on the hulls

A close-up view of a "cocoon" or "igloo" placed over a 5-inch/.38-caliber open-mount gun. This particular cover was aboard the USS *Hornet* (CVS-12), which had been saved from the shipbreakers after having been mothballed at the Puget Sound Naval Shipyard in Bremerton, Washington, for 20 years. This image was taken in the summer of 1999 at the Alameda Naval Air Station on San Francisco Bay where the *Hornet* is moored as a museum ship. *Author's collection by Sarah Lanzaro*

and eliminate salt air. Interestingly, when the *Iowa*-class battleship USS *Missouri* was to be transferred to Pearl Harbor, Hawaii, from the Puget Sound Naval Shipyard in 1998, it was decided that she should make a visit to Astoria, Oregon. The fresh water in the anchorage at Astoria would kill certain sea organisms contracted in Bremerton, Washington's, saltwater harbor. This layover was a treat for the people of Astoria, and helped preserve the ship in the ocean environment of Pearl Harbor. Other considerations for fleet storage were proximity to a shipyard, but distance from busy harbors. There had to be easy access to the fleet from the shore and the ability to openly observe the ships. Reduced opportunity of vandalism by intruders was also considered important. After all, who knew how long these ships might be laid up? A few still remained in the year 2000, and

Submarines are at rest at their base in New London, Connecticut, in 1946. Periscopes and propellers have been removed and stored. The engines have been preserved, and the electrolyte has been drained from the batteries. Dehumidifiers have been set up to keep the interior of the boats tight and dry. To the extreme right with the familiar "igloo" covering its 3-inch deck gun is the USS *Cavalla* (SS-244). This boat became famous when she discovered and radioed the position of the Japanese Fleet on June 17, 1944, and initiated the successful Battle of the Philippine Sea from June 19 to 20, 1944. On June 19, 1944, she sank the Japanese aircraft carrier IJN *Shokaku* during flight operations. This was one of the six December 7, 1941, Pearl Harbor attack veterans, and it was highly sought after. *U.S. Navy*

Plastic sheathing used to cover open 5-inch/.25-caliber guns on the light cruiser USS *Brooklyn* (CL-40) in early 1946. Plastic was just coming into use and the ability to cover a sensitive piece of machinery was important to its preservation. The *Brooklyn* was the first major ship mothballed. *Treasure Island Museum–SFCB*

one extraordinary use of these vessels was for grain storage in 1954. The U.S. Department of Agriculture was able to successfully store 72 million bushels of price-supported wheat in the holds of 317 *Liberty* ships.

The other major agency responsible for preserving a large number of vessels was the U.S. Navy. The determination as to the active force level was subject to much discussion and argument in the immediate years that followed the war. Between 1945 and 1950, when the Korean War changed the way politicians viewed the U.S. Navy, several proposals were made. The number of active major combatant ships at the end of the war was 1,079 vessels, including 27 fleet carriers, 89 smaller carriers, 18 battleships, 81 cruisers, 200 submarines, and 663 destroyer-type ships. This number was quickly reduced to 800 ships and has kept going down. After all, men were leaving the Navy, and the ability to maintain a combat fleet 75 percent of its wartime size with 25 percent of its wartime personnel was absurd. Despite the uncomfortable image of the Soviet Navy based on the bellicose statements of its leaders, the fleet size shrank faster than cotton in hot water. Officers and enlisted personnel whose livelihood depended on the retention of ships were worried, but political leaders and taxpayers were not. Aside from the mass scrapping that claimed hundreds of ships, vessels were entering preservation sites as quickly as they could be developed. It was further rationalized that the U.S. possession of nuclear arms and intercontinental-capable

These are the warning signs on the USS *Clamp* (ARS-33) in the Suisun Bay Reserve Fleet anchorage in October 1999. "No Trespassing U.S. Gov't Property-Violators will be prosecuted." Open anchorages are routinely patrolled to prevent vandalism and keep curiosity seekers from being injured. The salvage ship *Clamp* dates to World War II and shows her age with large pits in her hull plating. *Author's collection*

bombers would keep any potential enemy, mainly the Soviet Union, at bay.

Surface warships suffered the most, and the aircraft carriers were not spared. By 1949 the only battleship in commission was the USS *Missouri*, and she was being sailed with a vastly reduced complement as a training unit. The remaining battleships in the U.S. inventory, *North Carolina*-class (2), *South Dakota*-class (4), *California*-class (2), *Colorado*-class (3), and three of *Iowa*-class, have found reserve homes in the backwaters of naval shipyards. The State of Texas rescued its namesake battleship—USS *Texas* (BB-35), and she is currently a museum ship, the only reminder of the pre–World War II battleship experience.

The three large *Midway*-class aircraft carriers were essentially postwar units kept in commission, but the majority of the *Essex* class were mothballed along with the *Independence*-class light carriers, which originated from the *Cleveland*-class light cruiser hulls. Six of the *Essexes*, the namesake USS *Essex* (CV-9), USS *Ticonderoga* (CV-14), USS *Yorktown* (CV-10), USS *Lexington* (CV-16), USS *Bunker Hill* (CV-17), and USS *Bon Homme Richard* (CV-31), were laid up at the Puget Sound Naval Shipyard in Bremerton, Washington. Four *Essex*-class, four *Independence*-class, and four escort carriers (CVE) were kept in service between the end of World War II and the invasion of South. Seventy-five CVEs were demobilized—virtually en masse. Sixteen were docked at the Boston Navy Yard, including the USS *Rudyard Bay* (CVE-81), which remained a unit of the Atlantic Reserve Fleet from 1946 to 1959. As a counterpoint, sister ship USS *Solomons* (CVE-67) was decommissioned and stricken on the same day—June 5, 1946—and towed away for scrapping five months later. Aircraft from the *Solomons* were responsible for disposing of a U-boat on June 15, 1944, in the Atlantic.

Cruisers fared little better. All of the prewar light and heavy cruisers were laid up except those

This is one of hundreds of yard tenders and small craft built during World War II as ship service operatives. Two survive at the Philadelphia Naval Shipyard Inactive Ship Maintenance Facility (former Atlantic Reserve Fleet). The "V" barred flooding marker is visible near the port bow of the nearest vessel. Ships are checked daily to insure that they are not taking on water. *Author's collection*

This is the alarm warning light system for a nest of decommissioned destroyers at the Philadelphia Naval Shipyard. The upper lights (green) are lit to indicate no problem with the five ships in the moored group. The lights are hanging from the lifeline aboard the USS *Bigelow* (DD-942). *Author's collection*

Ships are protected in reserve sites, but so are the workers. This November 1999 photograph of the gangway between the decommissioned USS *Charles F Adams* (DDG-2) and USS *Sampson* (DDG-10) also shows a rope net slung under. It looks tattered like the ships, but would probably save a worker's life. The ships are moored in the Philadelphia Naval Shipyard. *Author's collection*

expended targets for Operation Crossroads, the USS *Pensacola* (CA-24), and USS *Salt Lake City* (CA-25). Of the war-built cruisers, most were mothballed with their older sisters at the Philadelphia and San Francisco Reserve Fleet sites. The *Cleveland*-class light cruiser USS *Galveston* (CL-93) literally went from the cradle to the grave as an all-gun cruiser. On June 24, 1946, she was mothballed in the Philadelphia Group of the Atlantic Reserve Fleet before she was completed. On May 28, 1958, she emerged as a missile cruiser and was finally commissioned as (CLG-3). She joined sisters USS *Little Rock* (CLG-4), which is now a memorial in Buffalo, New York, and USS *Oklahoma* City (CLG-5) was sunk as a target in June 1999.

Submarines found homes in the Napa River as far out of the way as possible at the Mare Island Naval Shipyard, and the Submarine Base at New London, Connecticut. The base expanded to accommodate mothballed veterans of World War II with nine new piers—up river.

As to destroyer-type vessels, there were 809 at the end of the war, but after scrapping or being surveyed out of service, the number was reduced to over 600. By 1948, the Navy had a total of 134 destroyers that were commissioned as units of the fleet. In reality, however, only 82 could be put to sea with sufficient crew to fight and return the ship to its base. It was hoped that the other 52 destroyers would not be called upon for immediate response. Nearly all of the decommissioned destroyers were placed in reserve sites at San Diego, Charleston, and Long Beach. Unlike the war a generation before, large numbers of destroyers did not haunt

Mooring chain lines are tied to the bottom of Suisun Bay to hold the ex-helicopter carriers USS *New Orleans* (LPH-11) and USS *Okinawa* (LPH-3) at the extreme end of a row of 15 large ships. Ships are first correctly and safely moored when placed in reserve fleet anchorages. Rarely has a ship broken loose, even in the worst weather. *Author's collection*

The light cruisers USS *Brooklyn* (CL-40) (pierside) and USS *Phoenix* (CL-46) after entering the Atlantic Reserve Fleet at Philadelphia. Both ships have been dry-docked, and the hulls are painted with antifouling compounds and are being dehumidified to keep them dry and tight. Five years after this March 1946 photograph was taken, both were sold to South American navies. *Treasure Island Museum–SFCB*

Cleveland-class light cruiser USS *Little Rock* (CL-92/CLG-4) is moored at her new home in Buffalo, New York, as a museum ship. She served in World War II and was laid up in the New York Group on June 24, 1949. She and other suitable *Cleveland*-class cruisers were brought out and refitted as missile cruisers (antiair) in the late 1950s. The *Little Rock* served until decommissioned in 1976 and was quickly saved by the City of Buffalo to become a museum ship. *Author's collection*

This is the San Francisco Group of the 19th Pacific Reserve Fleet in 1949. A large number of *Cleveland*-class cruisers is moored along with three *Essex*-class carriers. The battleship USS *Iowa* (BB-61) can be seen at the upper left of the photograph opposite a fast attack carrier and the yard's huge crane. Just seaward of the crane is the burned-out hulk of the light aircraft carrier *Independence*. Among the cruisers were the USS *Oklahoma City* (CL-91), USS *Vicksburg* (CL-86), and heavy cruisers USS *Bremerton* (CA-130) and USS *Los Angeles* (CA-135). The *Los Angeles* and *Bremerton* were members of the Hunters Point boneyard until the Korean War when their 8-inch guns were needed again for shore bombardment.
San Francisco Maritime Museum

the Philadelphia Naval Shipyard. That had become a de facto cruiser haven.

The impressive force of 362 destroyer escorts was reduced to 6 ships that were fully operational and 6 others that might be able to serve if a full crew could be provided. Periodically, these DEs were used by new officers for seamanship and ship-driving training, which accounted for a substantial number of dents and scrapes—as did the piers and buoys being approached! Many of the escorts were deactivated in Florida and others found their way to San Diego and Mare Island.

Virtually all of the U.S. Navy's amphibious force was either mothballed or sold off in the years before the outbreak of the Korean War. Those that were retained in reserve found good company with nearly new destroyers and destroyer escorts.

The light cruiser USS *Vicksburg* (CL-86) in happier days. The *Cleveland*-class cruiser is shown moored at Mare Island on October 26, 1946, celebrating Navy Day. In the background, the Mare Island ship repository is nearly at capacity and soon will have 106 of the fleet's submarine force. *Treasure Island Museum*

The USS *Enterprise* (CV-6), the most celebrated warship in contemporary U.S. Naval history, is shown as she is pushed from her reserve berth to Kearny, New Jersey, to be broken up for scrap metal. Tugs nudge the ship past the Brooklyn Bridge in this August 21, 1958, photograph. The *Enterprise* was sold to Lipsett, Inc. for $566,333.00, a sum that could not be raised by preservation groups. The Kearny location later played host to other carriers being scrapped: USS *Essex* (CV-9), USS *Boxer* (CV-21), USS *Wasp* (CV-7), USS *Antietam* (CV-36), and the *Midway*-class carrier USS *Franklin D Roosevelt* (CV-42). The "Big E" may have been the first, but she was not alone. The late 1950s and early 1960s represented the beginning of the end of the ships of World War II. *Treasure Island Museum–SFCB*

Initially, the ships that were immobilized were placed in groups as part of two reserve fleets. The 16th Fleet was the Atlantic Reserve and the 19th was the Pacific Reserve. Plans had been formulated in the latter part of World War II to accommodate an expected large number of demobilized warships. A total of 2,269 U.S. Navy vessels went into mothballs in the immediate years following World War II. Both the Maritime Commission and the U.S. Navy conceived ideas that would truly protect this expensive and valuable national asset—its Navy and service forces.

No More Red Lead—Mothballing and *Operation Zipper*

The Navy had easily identified the fallacies of the "red lead" approach simply by experience with the World War I–era flush deck destroyers that were reintroduced to the fleet in the late 1930s. The reports from the Royal Navy/Royal Canadian Navy after receiving the 50 ships were not encouraging. Simply putting a new paint on the exterior did not cure rust, leaks, rot, and corrosion that were the result of years of neglect and weak measures to preserve ships.

The *Cleveland*-class cruiser, USS *Santa Fe* (CL-60) is shown leaving its reserve fleet site for scrapping in this December 8, 1959, photograph. The *Santa Fe* fought through much of the Pacific campaign and was best remembered for pulling alongside the burning *Essex*-class carrier USS *Franklin* (CV-13) and rescuing 833 members of her crew. The carrier had been devastated by bombs and internal explosions during a Japanese air attack on March 14, 1945, and the bravery of the *Santa Fe*'s crew saved hundreds of lives. The well-worn cruiser was decommissioned on October 19, 1946, and spent the next 13 years in the Bremerton Group of the Pacific Reserve Fleet. *Treasure Island Museum–SFCB*

The battleships USS *California* (BB-44) (left) and sister USS *Tennessee* (BB-43) sit opposite one another as they are being scrapped in the October 21, 1959, photo. Both were damaged during the Pearl Harbor attack, resurrected, and rebuilt for war service. Both had entered the Atlantic Reserve Fleet at Philadelphia, and as technological progress bypassed them, they were 2 of the first major ships selected for disposal. They both ended up at the Patapsco Scrap Yard in Baltimore, Maryland. *Treasure Island Museum–SFCB*

The *Fletcher*-class destroyer, USS *The Sullivans* (DD-537) is being recommissioned out of the Pacific Reserve Fleet on July 6, 1951. Hundreds of well-wishers came to witness this sentiment-filled warship's return to active service. Four of her sisters are still in mothballs in the background, awaiting their turn. *Treasure Island Museum–SFCB*

A series of new procedures for ship preservation had been developed that enabled ships to be broken out of reserve and made ready for action within weeks rather than months. This was considered vital due to the expected nature of wars to come. Nuclear conflict was not about to pause several months while ships were being reconditioned for active service. The thought of another six-month period to recondition the ships between December 1941 and June 1942 was abhorrent. The government wisely decided to spend money to preserve its multi-billion-dollar assets. The first major combat ship to enter formal reserve status was the USS *Brooklyn* (CL-40), veteran of *Operation Torch* and the battles that punctured the "soft underbelly of Europe."

The process of storing ships was named "mothballing" or more formally, *Operation Zipper*. The media described it as "Uncle Sam Canning Warships." The *Brooklyn* began the mothball process on October 30, 1945, and she was formally placed in reserve, in commission, on January 31, 1946. The process to preserve the cruiser and the 2,200-plus ships to follow was scientific, well planned, and organized. It also evolved and became refined with experience. For instance, painting external surfaces above the waterline was found to be more cosmetic than valuable as an antideterioration technique.

A reduced crew from the Philadelphia Naval Shipyard first removed all perishable supplies, which were stored ashore, and secured portable equipment ashore or within the ship. Items taken off the ship included wet and dry batteries, paint, thinners, medical supplies, small arms, the ship's store stock, and even band instruments. Equipment not destined for warehouses ashore and other items that would be easily affected by sunlight and water were stored below decks. This was not done during the red lead fleet days, when wood, canvas, and other nonmetallic items were quickly destroyed or corroded beyond practical use. On the wooden decks that were exposed, an antidecay preservative was applied and monitored by the ship's custodians. Draining excess water was important, and holes were drilled to reduce standing water. On aircraft carriers that were

Not all warship boneyard alumni are scrapped or become museums; some are lost. The Mexican Navy's Pacific Fleet flagship *California* rests hard aground south of Rosarito Beach in Baja, California, on January 17, 1972. The fast transport USS *Belet* (APD-109) was retired to the reserve fleet base at Jacksonville, Florida, in 1945, where she sat until 1969. She and five other APDs were purchased by the Mexican Navy in December 1969. The *California* became a total loss, and her remains can be seen at low tide. *Author's collection*

mothballed, wooden flight decks were preserved in the same fashion, and all external apertures were sealed against water leaks.

Detailed records were kept of all actions and a log book (or books) was set up for the ship to facilitate mobilization, if necessary. All compartments were thoroughly cleaned, and a major effort was made to remove any flaking rust or corrosion. Paint was liberally applied to those surfaces that needed it.

Each compartment was sealed with a dehumidifier installed to reduce the "airborne level of ambient water vapor." Basically, the key to preserving the Navy's ships was to keep them dry and tight. Metal corrosion, rot, mildew, and rust can be vastly reduced if the dehumidification process is properly maintained. A relative humidity of 25 to 30 percent and temperature levels were maintained by the system. In addition, preservative coatings were applied to sensitive areas and machinery that was prone to corrosion. The system also included methods to eradicate pests and rodents during lay-up periods.

All exterior openings in the ships were sealed with blank flanges, and cocoonlike metal shells were bolted over exposed gun mounts. Smokestack covers were installed, and all antennae and directors were removed and stowed below decks. A plastic coating was sprayed over items including open 5-inch/.25-caliber guns. First the item was draped with plastic sheathing and then sprayed with a liquid plastic until completely sealed. Air was removed from the enclosure to create a vacuumlike effect.

Alarm systems were implanted in areas throughout the ships to alert the custodial staff to leakage or intruders. To determine if water was entering the ship, alarms including counterweighted Styrofoam balls were placed in strategic points throughout the ship. The weight was placed on the top of the ball

and if it turned over due to water flooding, an alarm sounded, and caused a team to arrive quickly and remedy the problem. Flooding markers were also painted on the ship hulls and/or rudders. The marker was a "V" with three lines crossing through—it is luminous white in color, and its bottom was at the inactive ship waterline. It is 31 inches in height, and painted on the ship's port and starboard bow, and stern. These markers warned of any leakage and were to be continuously monitored.

Particular attention was paid to engineering spaces. Lubricant levels were inspected and brought up to standard. Pipes were drained of all water and fluid systems were treated with preservatives. Tags were dated and placed in specific areas to inform custodial or reactivation personnel of actions taken and when.

In the early days of the mothballing program, ships were assigned trained naval personnel as custodians that would protect their assigned ship from danger. When the *Brooklyn* went into reserve, her assigned crew consisted of 5 officers ands 59 enlisted men. Eventually, a well-developed personnel system was developed in the 16th and 19th Fleets to supervise the protection of the ships. The number of personnel assigned declined with the introduction of better monitoring methods and by the 1960s a small staff could watch over a large number of ships.

As part of the inactivation process, ships were placed in drydock and a thick preservative of antifouling paint was applied to the hull under the waterline. This meant that the ships had to rotate through dry-docking periods every two to five years. This aspect of the mothballing program became labor intensive and was not actually doing a proper job to preserve the ship. The hull plates were still pitting. It was not until the "cathodic protection system" was

The light cruiser USS *Amsterdam* (CL-101) is moored next to sister USS *Astoria* (CL-90) (left) and antiaircraft light cruiser USS *Tucson* (CLAA-98) (near right) in San Diego in September 1970. All of these ships were stricken and broken up the following year. In the case of the *Tucson*, she had been in reserve since 1949 with a brief period of service as a test hulk from 1966 through 1970. *Courtesy L. Cote*

of suspended impressed current anodes. It had been determined that natural electrolic action on exposed metal caused unrelenting corrosion. Anodes suspended underwater near the ship's hull helped neutralize electrochemical action. The cathodic protection system helped prevent this action. It consisted of four key items: 1. anodes—various metallic units were used, and after 1983, a 0.1-inch thick niobium wire thinly coated with platinum that could be cut to desired lengths; 2. power supply (conventional AC power rectified to DC, which was distributed through anodes to the underwater portion of a ship's hull); 3. current distribution system; 4. reference electrode (determines current levels on hull surfaces). Periodic underwater inspections by divers were also part of the method used to preserve hull integrity.

The condition of the cathodic protection equipment as well as the underwater hull surface was continuously monitored. At first, a cabled grid system was developed for ships in rows to be moored over. This proved unworkable, and a method was developed to suspend anodes (metallic lengths of wire) alongside ships that were laid up. This worked quite well, and in 1960 a further improvement came with the change to graphite anodes. Nests of ships could be protected corporately or a single ship could be subjected to this system.

In 1983, anodes were further evolved with the conversion to platinum-niobium. In this system, a platinum-clad niobium wire anode (5-foot wire) was suspended alongside the hull, and the current flowing into it had to remain at 0.5 ampere or above to maintain a brittle brownish peroxide coating. This coating protects the anode. It was further determined that the number of anodes is dependent on the condition of the hull and area where the ship is stored. For large vessels with 120,000-plus square feet of underwater surface with adequately coated anodes, in fresh or brackish water, 60 anodes are required. For the same ship and same anode condition in seawater, 24 anodes are required. Ideally, the current distributed throughout the hull on a continuous basis should be 0.80 volts. If too little voltage is used, the hull corrodes; if too much voltage is used, the hull paint will

developed and implemented that the underwater surface was assured the best possible safeguarding. Prior to the implementation of the cathodic protection system, zinc or magnesium plates were used to retard corrosion. These were galvanic anodes and considered sacrificial in that they corroded in place of the hull. However, this method proved less than satisfactory.

In 1957, the process changed with the introduction of the cathodic protection system that consisted

This is a rear view of cruisers *Amsterdam* (left) and *Astoria* (right) while in the San Diego inactive ship facility September 1970. Dehumidification hoses in various apertures in the ships to maintain low ambient water vapor in the interiors can easily be seen from this aspect. Stack covers are on the funnels, all antennae are stored below decks, and gun sleeves are sealed against moisture. Keeping the vessel tight is essential to preservation. *Courtesy L. Cote*

be damaged. The system began to show results immediately. Vessels that normally were slated for dry-docking every two to five years were safe in the water for 15 to 20 years.

Other details in hull inactivation included covering external sea connections with flanges on the outside of the hull, securing all portholes, and placing locking devices on rudders and props. As environmental concerns became more evident, measures were taken to protect the water basin where the ship was mothballed. This included floating a yellow or red oil boom around the vessel or nest of vessels if they were in a confined water body such as Puget Sound in Philadelphia.

The USS *Brooklyn* (CL-40) was the first of many ships to be placed in reserve. A rather novel ceremony took place for the *Brooklyn* on January 30, 1946. Admiral T. C. Kincaid, commander of the 16th Fleet, threw a switch to initiate

dehumidification in the last compartment of the *Brooklyn* and she was sealed. Another 2,268 ships would follow, including the old heavy cruiser USS *Chester* (CA-27). Over the next five years, the majority of the fleet found its way into mothballs and attached to one group or another.

The U.S. Navy formed Reserve Units nationwide to keep pace with training and changes in ships and weapons. Like their former ships, the Navy Reserve was prepared to fight on short notice.

From accounting and taxpayer value viewpoints, $13 billion in military hardware, and a similar value in merchant shipping, was satisfactorily stored for just under $100 million—less than the cost of one new aircraft carrier. Of course, the ships placed in reserve between 1946 and 1950 would not last forever, but the existence of these fading gray veterans gave notice to the world that the U.S. Navy could respond if the need arose. The need came sooner than expected.

The troop- and cargo-carrying submarine USS *Perch* (LPSS–313) (amphibious transport submarine) went through a number of configurations during her 26-year career. In the main, she was a commando insertion unit and forerunner to the U.S. Navy's request to have four *Trident* submarines converted for this purpose in the early twenty-first century. The 312-foot-long *Balao*-class World War II–era submarine *Perch* is seen at the San Diego facility in 1971. She was sold and broken up the following year. *Courtesy L. Cote*

Perhaps one of the most famous inhabitants of any warship boneyard has been the odd-looking and mysterious CIA-sponsored Hughes Glomar Explorer as seen in this July 1997 photograph at the Suisun Bay Reserve Fleet anchorage. She was used to covertly raise part of a sunken Soviet Golf II-class ballistic missile submarine in 1974. From 1980 until 1998, she was a familiar sight in Suisun Bay; however, she was refitted and at present mines the ocean floor for minerals like her original cover story indicated. Author's collection

Chapter Eight

THE KOREAN CONFLICT AND VIETNAM WAR

1950–1975

On June 25, 1950, North Korean troops poured across their southern border and invaded the Republic of Korea. It was the first major test of the United Nations and the resolve of the United States to prevent the spread of Communist aggression. The active U.S. Navy was ill prepared to defend South Korea against the land assault, and fortunately there was little North Korean naval capability. The invasion caused the deployment of all the U.S. surface ships in the area and the available aircraft carriers (USS *Philippine Sea* [CVA-47] and USS *Valley Forge* [CVA-45]). More combatants would appear on the scene, but for the moment the naval forces in the war zone consisted of the

The Korean War graphically demonstrated to the American public and the world the wisdom of preserving its navy. More than 500 ships were withdrawn from boneyards to bolster the fleet. Here the light carrier USS *Monterrey* (CVL-26) is being prepared for recommissioning in Philadelphia on February 2, 1951. In the background can be seen *Brooklyn-St Louis*-class cruisers in mothballs. *Treasure Island Museum —SFCB*

Restocking the interior with just the basics was a supply officer's nightmare, and modern electronic equipment was often installed. Engineering plants had to be made ready and a competent crew selected. The 30-day reactivation plan was just that—a plan. Overall, the reactivation of hundreds of ships went much smoother than expected.

It was almost a who's who of *Fletcher* class when the USS *Trathen* (DD-530), USS *Boyd* (DD-544), USS *Jarvis* (DD-799), and USS *Walke* (DD-723) came to Korea to assist in the United Nations effort. The *Walke* did double duty. She was hit by a floating mine on June 12, 1951, that did substantial damage and killed 26 crew members. Repaired at the Mare Island Naval Shipyard, she returned to the war zone a year later in June 1952. Not all destroyers brought out of mothballs were deployed to the Western Pacific. Many were assigned to the Atlantic and Mediterranean Fleets to bolster their presence in the emerging Cold War with the Soviet Union.

cruiser USS *Juneau* (CLAA-119), two Royal Navy cruisers, and destroyers such as the USS *DeHaven* (DD-727), USS *Mansfield* (DD-728), USS *Fletcher* (DD-445), and the ubiquitous USS *Maddox* (DD-731).

Soon, the U.S. forces were joined by carriers USS Oriskany (CVA-34), USS *Boxer* (CVA-21), and USS *Princeton* (CVA-37). All four *Iowa*-class battleships came and fought in the war zone, as did a number of cruisers including the USS *Helena* (CA-75) and USS *St. Paul* (CA-73). Destroyers and destroyer escorts came out of mothballs in droves and prepared for battle.

The reactivation process was not as easy as originally planned. Ships had to be dry-docked and repainted, and all of the exterior equipment needed to be reinstalled.

In Bayonne, New Jersey, the state's namesake, USS *New Jersey* (BB-62) has a metal igloo removed from a 40mm antiaircraft gun mount. The *Iowa*-class battleship, shown here on September 26, 1950, was slated to replace the USS *Missouri* (BB-63) as a training ship. The *Missouri* had been deployed to Korea. *Treasure Island Museum—SFCB*

By the end of the war, the United Nations effort at sea, led by the U.S. Navy, established and maintained a siege on the port of Wonsan in North Korea that lasted 861 days. The U.S. Navy could not have achieved this or any of the other major contributions to the war (Inchon amphibious landings, carrier air support, and naval bombardment of shore targets) without hundreds of ships emerging from the mothball fleet. The warship boneyard of World War II spawned 665 warships during the three-year conflict. The Navy employed 575 vessels in the war, and many came from San Diego, Suisun Bay, Charleston, and Philadelphia reserve centers. The men that came with these ships returned to active duty five years after fighting what they had been hoped to be the last war in their lives. The lawyers, construction workers, college professors, and good working men and women of the United States again did a creditable job.

A few of the ships returned to hibernation after the end of the conflict, but a new war had become evident. The Cold War had begun, and the U.S. Navy, which was slated for just 324 active vessels, now had 1,066 vessels, including 194 destroyers.

During the 1950s, ships came and went into storage. Several were sold outright to friendly foreign powers under the terms of the Mutual Defense Assistance Program. For 10 percent of the original price plus renovation costs, countries could purchase relatively new warships at bargain prices. Six *Brooklyn-St Louis*-class cruisers were sold to South American nations—two each went to Chile, Argentina, and Brazil. The *Brooklyn* became the Chilean *Crucero O'Higgins*. Destroyers, destroyer escorts, submarines, and amphibious ships were sold off or lent to countries like Greece, Turkey, Italy, Holland, and Vietnam. Three *Independence*-class light carriers were loaned or sold. The USS *Cabot* (CVL-28) went to Spain, the USS *Belleau Wood* (CVL-24) came out of mothballs at the Alameda Naval Air Station and went to France in 1953 to join the USS *Langley* (CVL-27).

A view of the Hunters Point (San Francisco Group) inactive ship facility in the mid-1950s. In the foreground is the USS *Vincennes* (CL-64), USS *Amsterdam* (CL-101), and the escort carrier USS *Sitkoh Bay* (CVE-86). Special attention was paid to the wooden decks of the carriers, and they were periodically sprayed with preservatives. Still, the ravages of weather took their toll. The USS *Sicily* (CVE-118) is moored across from the *Sitkoh Bay*. The escort carrier served three tours in Korea before being decommissioned in 1954.
San Francisco Maritime Museum

Several destroyer escorts were removed from reserve fleet anchorages and converted to mid-ocean radar picket sentries (early warning). In Pearl Harbor on July 28, 1965, 3 of the 34 *Edsall*-class ships that were rebuilt were moored alongside "bravo" pier. The USS *Kretchmer* (DER-329), USS *Camp* (DER-251), and USS *Hissem* (DER-400) have trainable forward-throwing hedgehog ASW armament and two radar-controlled rapid-fire 3-inch/.50-guns. During the 1950s they were successful adjuncts to the overall defense of the nation, and destined for retirement in the early 1960s. However, they went on to enforce the blockade of arms traffic off Vietnam (Operation MarketTime) throughout the 1960s. Their endurance and crew habitability were ideal for long patrols along the Vietnamese coast. *U.S. Navy*

The USS *Sailfish* (SSR-572) quietly sits under the port flight deck overhang of the aircraft carrier USS *Midway* (CVA-41) at the Puget Sound Naval Shipyard in July 1997. She is one of the few conventionally powered submarines left in the United States. The *Sailfish* was commissioned on July 9, 1956, and was originally destined for radar picket in the frenzy of the 1950s, fear of Soviet air attack. The *Sailfish* was converted to an attack configuration in 1961 and retired to Bremerton in 1977. Like dozens of surface ships, the *Sailfish* has rested in a warship boneyard for decades. *Author's collection*

Many ships were withdrawn from the reserve fleets for specialized purposes such as radar picket duty and to fulfill the increasing need for antisubmarine warfare due to perceptions of a dangerous Soviet submarine force. Chronologically new destroyer escorts were considered quite suitable for modification to these tasks.

Those selected for radar picket (DER) duty were modified to occupy lonely spaces in the ocean and electronically search for Soviet aircraft or warships. From Mare Island, destroyers, destroyer escorts, and submarines came out of mothballs during the 1950s. The USS *Hissem* (DE-400/DER-400) was recommis-

sioned August 31, 1956, and was modified for DER, and the *Fletcher*-class destroyer USS *O'Bannion* (DD-450) emerged as an ASW escort (DDE) on February 19, 1951, in tandem with sister USS *Nicholas* (DD-449) on the same day. Both came back to the Mare Island warship boneyard in the early 1970s along with the *Hissem*.

The Navy needed its World War II-era submarines for patrolling and carrying troops, as hauling tankers, and to use for an upgrade under the greater underwater propulsion (GUPPY) system. Boats, such as the *Lionfish* (SS-298), *Perch* (SSP-313), *Barbero* (SS-317), and *Batfish* (SS-310) were recommissioned.

Now described as an Inactive Ship Maintenance Facility, this is the San Diego reserve fleet as it looked in July 1969. To the far left is the stern of the USS *Begor* (APD-127), a fast transport conversion from a destroyer escort. She remained in the facility from 1962 until she was transferred to Indonesia in 1975. Across the channel is the USS *Arlington* (AGMR-2), a communication ship that was formerly the USS *Saipan* (CVL-48). She was stricken in 1975, a year after the USS *Kearsarge* (CV-33) (right) was broken up. *Courtesy L. Cote*

The late 1950s and early 1960s witnessed the end of an era as one ship after another was purged from mothball fleets on both coasts. Ships like the USS *Enterprise* (CV-6), were towed away to be scrapped. The year 1959 became one of the most devastating years for the older ships when 45 major combatants were approved for sale to the scrappers. The light cruisers USS *Honolulu* (CL-48) and USS *Savannah* (CL-42) were joined by the heavy cruisers USS *San Francisco* (CA-38) and USS *Wichita* (CA-45), and the battleships were not spared. The USS *California* (BB-44), sister USS *Tennessee* (BB-43) and USS *West Virginia* (BB-48) were approved for sale and were followed by others, including the USS *South Dakota* (BB-57) and USS *Indiana* (BB-59), within two years.

There were renewed requests from individual Congress members to consider breaking up the four *Iowa*-class battleships, especially considering the new Navy that was moving into the nuclear and guided-missile age. Many forward-thinking naval officers and Congressional members cried, "the gun was dead." Reserve organizations and pro-battleship sponsors won the battle. The *Iowa* class was to be spared—at least temporarily. The $50,000 annual maintenance fee was not astronomical.

When the Navy and National Defense Reserve Fleet were quickly reducing the size of their boneyards, 15- to 20-year-old *Liberty* and *Victory* ships by the score were towed away and broken up. The cost to maintain so many quickly obsolescing ships was too great, and the money was needed elsewhere for new construction. The necessity for retaining many of the surviving ships was questioned when military and political leaders pondered the use of strategic nuclear weapons. What good would it do to have ships in reserve when all that would be left after an exchange of atomic bombs with the Soviet Union would be rubble and a nuclear wasteland?

The Crisis- and War-Laden 1960s

The U.S. Navy was called upon for help numerous times after the decision had been made to scrap many of the ships in its reserve inventory. Ships continued to enter and re-enter the Reserve Fleets, including many heavy cruisers such as the USS *Los Angeles* (CA-135), the USS *Toledo* (CA-133), and the USS *Bremerton* (CA-130). Many

Essex-class aircraft carrier USS *Kearsarge* (CV-33) returns astronaut Wally Schirra from the Mercury program and his space capsule to Pearl Harbor in October 1962. Sailors line the rail in salute to the United States and its navy for the obvious strides in the U.S. space exploration program. Eight years later, after American astronauts landed on the moon, the old carrier was decommissioned and laid up in San Diego. *Author's collection*

The heavy cruiser USS *Toledo* (CA-133) at the San Diego facility on September 17, 1970. She is moored next to the USS *Galveston* (CLG-3), a *Cleveland*-class light cruiser conversion to a missile ship. The *Galveston* was a recent addition and had only been mothballed for five months. The *Toledo* (the more faded ship) had been in residence since May 21, 1960. A full decade in reserve and the *Toledo* still looked quite good.
Courtesy L. Cote

ships had been employed in the Korean War and there seemed to be an abundance of all gun warships in the fleet. The missile cruiser and destroyer had come to stay.

The Cuban Missile Crisis in October 1962 caused a large number of warships to again be brought out of mothballs and many ships that were slated for the boneyards remained active. There was also unrest in the Pacific. The Vietnam War, which had been brewing in Southeast Asia for years, began to perceptively escalate in 1964 when the USS *Maddox* (DD-731) and USS *C. Turner Joy* (DD-951) were parties to North Vietnamese aggression in the Gulf of Tonkin during August 2 through 4 of that year. Coincidentally, the destroyer *Maddox* seemed to be a common thread of naval warfare in Asia since World War II. She was on station at the beginning of the Korean War and again present at the outset of the new war.

These 8-inch guns of the *Toledo* are plugged and covered with faded paint. The *Toledo*, which served as a reserve warrior in 1970, had fired on Communist targets in North Korea on August 20, 1951. The heavy cruiser was eventually stricken on January 1, 1974, and sold for scrap on October 30, 1974.
Treasure Island Museum–SFCB

The war in Southeast Asia required aircraft carriers and cruisers, but mostly destroyers and transport vessels were needed. Destroyers that had been modified for ASW work found themselves using what few 5-inch/.38-caliber guns they had left for inshore bombardment. Cruisers that had been altered to carry Talos missiles as their main battery were pressed into service for their 6- and 8-inch guns. The USS *Oklahoma City* (CLG-5) was joined by the USS *Canberra* (CAG-2) to provide fire support for ground

The Korean War veteran USS *Philippine Sea* (CV-47*)* steams under the San Francisco Bay Bridge in this early 1950s photograph. Her air group includes F9F Panther jets (abaft the island), F4U Corsair fighters, and AD4 Skyraiders (aft). This *Essex*-class carrier was not modernized with an angled flight deck or other improvements to handle modern jet aircraft and ended her days when she was scrapped in 1970. *Author's collection*

The aviation transport USS *Philippine Sea* (AVT-11, formerly CV-47) is at rest in San Diego on September 17, 1970. The *Philippine Sea* had flown strikes in Korea and in 1958 was decommissioned and placed in reserve. The following year she was redesignated an AVT. The aft 6-inch/.47-caliber gun turrets of the USS *Amsterdam* (CL-101*)* are in the foreground. *Courtesy L. Cote*

The heavy cruiser USS *Los Angeles* (CA-135) is shown at the San Diego inactive ship maintenance facility in September 1970. To her left is the flight deck overhang of the USS *Philippine Sea* (AVT-11). A cocoon covers her forward twin 3-inch/.50-caliber antiaircraft guns, but her wooden deck is beginning to look quite weathered after being laid up since 1963. *Courtesy L. Cote*

forces, and in 1967 the battleship USS *New Jersey* (BB-62) was pulled out of mothballs and modified for service in Southeast Asia. Her 16-inch guns were needed, and on September 29, 1968, she was back on duty shelling enemy targets.

Several destroyer escorts, which had been modified for radar picket duty (DER), were deployed for coastal patrol off Vietnam. Most had been slated for mothballs, but their particular configuration was judged ideal for patrol work. The USS *Camp* (DER-251), had the most varied career. Commissioned in 1943 as an *Edsall*-class destroyer escort, she fought in World War II until she was mothballed in 1946. Reactivated in 1956, she was reconfigured as a DER. She operated in the North Atlantic and off the coast of Vietnam until 1970, when she was transferred to the South Vietnamese Navy in 1971 as the *Tran Hung Dao*. After the war ended, she was purchased by the Republic of the Philippines and renamed the *Rajah Lakandula* in 1976. She served as that navy's most powerful warship into the 1990s.

Despite the yearly decline in the number of cargo vessels in the National Defense Reserve Fleet (NDRF), its vessels continued to be recalled for military service. With the 540 ships called during the Korean War, the NDRF contributed 172

Destroyers USS *Herbert J Thomas* (DD-833), USS *Albert W. Grant* (DD-649), and USS *Henry A. Wiley* (DM-29) are moored together at the San Diego inactive ship maintenance facility in 1971. The *Thomas,* which had been converted to a radar picket sentry, was sold to Taiwan three years after this photograph was taken and renamed the *Han Yang.* The other two tin cans were broken up the following year. *Courtesy L. Cote*

The photographer, Larry Cote of Stockton, California, endangered his life to shoot this picture of the Mare Island Inactive Ship Maintenance Facility on May 23, 1972. In the foreground is a World War II–vintage barrack ship, APL-3. In the background is the mothballed submarine tender USS *Nereus* (AS-17). In 1920, these docks were crowded with flush deck destroyers; in 1950, dozens of submarines; and in 1972, the remnants of World War II plus some of the early postwar construction. *Courtesy L. Cote*

Destroyers, destroyer escorts, and LSTs are moored together in the muddy waters of the Napa River at Mare Island in May 1972. The World War II and Korean War veteran USS *Owen* (DD-536) had been moored at the Stockton facility from 1958 through 1970. She moved to Mare Island a year after the photograph, and was broken up along with scores of other former World War II ships that technology had long since left behind. *Courtesy L. Cote*

Four *Agile*-class minesweepers moored at Mare Island in May 1972. These wooden-hulled boats were designed during the Korean War and displaced 750 tons full load. Several ended their days in the Spanish and Philippine navies. The USS *Advance* (MSO-510) was active from 1956 through 1970 and stricken in 1976. There was some thought given to modernizing these fine boats; however, the advent of helicopter minesweeping techniques rendered them obsolete. *Courtesy L. Cote*

vessels during the Vietnam era. Ironically, the ships were in reasonably good condition, but after 20 years, it was becoming increasingly difficult to find spare parts and shipmates who were familiar with the eccentricities of the World War II *Liberty* and *Victory* ships. By the mid-1960s the NDRF still had a total of 1,327 vessels, but by 1975 that number had been slashed to 419.

In 1965, the U.S. Navy now had 600 ships in its six Reserve Fleet Groups: Bremerton, Washington; Mare Island/Stockton, and San Diego, California; Orange, Texas; Norfolk, Virginia; and Philadelphia, Pennsylvania. This was slightly more than one quarter of its highest number in 15 years. The Philadelphia Naval Shipyard played host to 122 ships, and the overall number of ships continued to shrink because the World War II ships were aging. Great Britain's Royal Navy now had an active fleet of 143 ships, and its boneyards mostly held ships in transition from active to being scrapped. The world's navies left over from World War II had nearly vanished in just two decades. A small number

of ships were saved from the scrapper's torch by private groups that wanted to preserve naval heritage. The battleships USS *North Carolina* (BB-55), USS *Massachusetts* (BB-59), and USS *Alabama* (BB-60) were established as memorials in their states by 1965.

By 1970, much of the American public had become vocally opposed to the war in Southeast Asia, and the first of the decade's defense cutbacks, reduced the active fleet of 850 ships by 158 units. This included the battleship *New Jersey* and *Essex*-class aircraft carriers USS *Yorktown* (CVS-10), USS *Hornet* (CVS-12), and USS *Kearsarge* (CVS-33). Several of the old *Fletcher*-, *Gearing*-, and *Sumner*-class destroyers that were once considered the backbone of the Navy were decommissioned and mothballed, scrapped, or sold to other nations. Most of the older submarines had already been disposed of and there was little need for an excessive number of tenders. The USS *Nereus* (AS-17), which had been built at Mare Island, was in mothballs by 1971. Other auxiliaries and tenders were also laid up or

This is a unique view of the number two turret of the USS *Bremerton* (CA-130) as the ship is being cut up for scrap at Zidell's Tacoma Yard on September 19, 1974. This is where it ends for the majority of warships. The barrels are cut off and the hulls are reduced to manageable chunks of good steel that can be reshaped into consumer products. *Courtesy L. Cote*

disposed of. The ships of World War II were now a quarter-century or more in age and all but worn out. The Navy again donated veteran ships as museum ships, such as the aircraft carrier *Yorktown* and submarines USS *Silversides* (SS-236) and USS *Ling* (SS-297). Veterans groups and the public at large did not want to repeat the same bitter experience that occurred with the senseless loss of the USS *Enterprise* (CV-6).

The mine force was not exempt, and many of the 1950s-built *Agile*-class minesweepers were laid up, including the USS *Advance* (MSO-510) and the namesake, the USS *Agile* (MSO-421).

The Vietnam War ended in 1975, and reductions in the navy and maritime fleet continued. The military and the navy were on the ebb with public approval—the warship boneyards were again filling up to capacity.

Mirror image Knox-class frigates are in reserve at the inactive ship site at Bremerton, Washington, in August 1998. From front to back are the USS Frances Hammond (FF-1067), USS Knox (FF-1052), USS Hepburn (FF-1055), and USS Roark (FF-1053). These ships were built to fill the need for ASW escorts to protect the supply route from the United States to other NATO countries in the event of war with the Soviet Union. By most accounts, they were unsatisfactory sea boats and their 27-knot speed precluded them from keeping pace with the fast carriers. Author's collection

Chapter Nine
TO THE NEXT MILLENNIUM

1975–2000

The possession of a massive and diverse reserve fleet that could be activated upon demand was a potent tool in the U.S. arsenal. The first real use was in the Korean War (1950–1953), and without a rapidly expanding naval force, the outcome might have been different for the United States. Activating and reactivating warships and auxiliaries proved to be a definite asset to the power projection of the United States; however, it was most effective for the conflicts that occurred during the 25 years after the end of World War II. The years took their toll, and it soon became apparent that mobilizing a reserve fleet of obsolescing ships had it limits. The ships were aging, and naval combat was evolving into the age of automation and guided missiles. This became most evident in the type of warfare being waged during the Cold War, and the level of technology required to prevail in modern naval combat. For example, World War II–built destroyers were sent to the Pacific to fight Japanese surface units and provide concentrated antiaircraft defense for the fast carriers. Antisubmarine warfare was considered to be a secondary mission. The Cold War brought ASW to the forefront. What the Navy needed were destroyer-type vessels to serve as long-range ASW escorts and hunters/killers. The *Fletcher-*, *Gearing-*, and *Sumner-*class destroyers, that had performed so well during World War II, had become "mission obsolete," and would remain so until they were upgraded.

Inability to adapt to new technology involving vessel size limitations and the hard service while on active duty quickly rendered large numbers of World War II–era ships obsolete. Ships that were built in the mid-1940s, and based on late-1930s designs, had inborn perimeters to their performance. This applied to virtually every ship type in the U.S. Navy, including the *Essex-*class aircraft carrier.

These were fine vessels, but as combat aircraft grew in size, the need for super carriers became increasingly evident. The dictum "more was better" in relation to size was clearly expressed in nearly every vessel classification.

The *Gearing-*class destroyer displaced a maximum of 3,500 tons full load on a 390-foot hull, and its mid–Cold War successor, the *Spruance* class, displaced 7,800 tons on a 563-foot overall length. The *Buckley-*class destroyer escort displaced 2,000 tons full load on a 306-foot overall length, yet its Cold War sister, the *Oliver Hazard Perry-*class, displaced 3,710 tons on a 445-foot overall length. Weapons systems and the need for shipboard space to accommodate electronics required larger vessels.

The *Gato* and *Balao* classes of World War II attack submarines displaced 2,424 tons submerged on a 312-foot-long hull compared to the *Los Angeles* class from 1970, which displaced a hefty 6,927 tons on a 360-foot-long hull. Both were attack submarines, but the *Los Angeles* class was far more capable and versatile. A submarine of the *Los Angeles-*class caliber was needed to locate and destroy Soviet ballistic missile submarines, a type of warfare not

Three destroyers are tied to the south pier at Mare Island in May 1972. Easily identifiable due to the cocoons on the 40mm antiaircraft guns in front of the bridge and abaft smokestack number two. Outboard is the USS *Norman Scott* (DD-690), which has been in reserve since 1946. The *Scott* never was upgraded and her mast is a dead giveaway. *Fletcher*-class destroyers were later crowded with electronics and required a tripod mast to bear the load. The *Scott* and her two sisters have pole masts. The *Scott* was the star of a World War II RKO-Pathe film entitled *This Is America – Navy Yard. Courtesy L. Cote*

The *Cleveland*-class light cruiser (first commissioned on December 22, 1944) turned guided missile ship USS *Oklahoma City* (CL-91/CLG-5) moored at the Suisun Bay Reserve Fleet anchorage in July 1997. The "OK City" was decommissioned and placed in the San Francisco Group of the Pacific Reserve Fleet on June 30, 1947. She was withdrawn 10 years later and was serving as a missile cruiser in the Pacific Fleet in 1960. Nineteen years later she was stricken, and until 1992 was moored at the Bremerton Reserve Fleet site. From 1992 until 1997 she was an electronic target ship for the weapons test center at Port Hueneme, California. She was transferred to the Suisun Bay site in 1996, and in June 1999, was sunk as a target by a South Korean submarine. Her 55-year career was varied. *Author's collection*

even conceived of during World War II. Simply withdrawing ships from reserve was not the answer to the increasingly modern and expanding Soviet Navy.

As early as 1960, it had become apparent that the U.S. Navy was unable to build new ships fast enough to meet existing commitments that were being faced with World War II units. Stopgap measures such as the Fleet Rehabilitation and Modernization (FRAM) program were introduced to extend the service life of the most needed classes of destroyers, cruisers, and aircraft carriers. It was soon discovered that there was a limited amount of space available for updated electronics, helicopters, and missiles aboard the older hulls. Even the ships that had been completely rebuilt for modern warfare, the USS *Albany* (CG-10), USS *Chicago* (CG-11), and USS *Oklahoma City* (CLG-5), were becoming obsolete by the mid-1970s.

The reason why one ship is kept in a warship boneyard when hundreds of her contemporaries and those built after her have been disposed of is sometimes difficult to understand. The USS *Clamp* (ARS-33), a World War II salvage tug, has been sitting in one Northern California port or another (now it is at Suisun Bay) since 1963 when she was formally stricken from the naval register. She was originally commissioned on August 23, 1943, and placed in mothballs on May 6, 1947. Her hull is pitted and worn, but in this October 1999 photograph, she is still afloat. *Author's collection*

The *Fletcher*-class destroyer USS *Cassin Young* (DD-793) is now a museum ship. Dedicated destroyer loyalists preserve these reminders of years past, and with the Navy's cooperation, they have secured a number of the World War II destroyers to be displayed for generations to come. *Author's collection*

Fletcher-class destroyers USS *Caperton* (DD-650), USS *Gatling* (DD-671), USS *Miller* (DD-535), USS *Hazelwood* (DD-531), and USS *Cassin Young* (DD-793) sit together at the Reserve Fleet basin in the Philadelphia Naval Shipyard. All except the *Cassin Young* were broken up within the next two years. The *Cassin Young* became a museum ship. *U.S.N.I.*

The heavy cruiser USS *Pittsburgh* (CA-72) awaits the shipbreaker's torch at Zidell's Yard in Tacoma, Washington, in this September 19, 1974, photograph. The cranes on the pier adjacent to the *Pittsburgh* will be used to lift large chunks of metal from the ship as she becomes a hulk. As is evident in this image, most scrapyards are in out-of-the-way areas of major harbors. *Courtesy L. Cote*

Traditional warfare at sea was slipping into history. Gun and torpedo dueling between lines of opposing cruisers and destroyers was a practice considered comparable to repelling boarders by the early 1970s. All gun cruisers such as the USS *Los Angeles* (CA-135) and USS Pittsburgh (CA-72) had been, or were going to be, sold for scrap. The *Des Moines* class of all gun super cruisers was laid up at the Philadelphia inactive ship maintenance facility beginning in 1961. For one reason or another, the

The USS *Des Moines* (CA-134) sits at Pier F at the Inactive Ship Maintenance Facility in the Philadelphia Naval Shipyard in November 1999. The old all-gun cruiser has been in residence there since her decommissioning on July 14, 1961. She is still in remarkably good condition, although the lack of sophisticated antennae and missile launchers betray her as a ship from another era. The future of this vessel was unclear at the time of the photograph, although there is a strong sentiment not to break her up for scrap. The partially dismantled USS *Harry E. Yarnell* (CG-17) was moored to her starboard side and is hidden by the old cruiser's superstructure. *Author's collection*

three ships survived the massive purges that reduced the numbers of vessels in the navy's warship boneyards. Of the three ships, the USS *Salem* (CA-139) became a museum ship in 1994, the USS *Newport News* (CA-148) was finally sold for scrap in 1993, and the oldest resident, the USS *Des Moines* (CA-134), which was decommissioned on July 14, 1961, was still in residence as of November 2000. This was an anomaly in the system, because with the exception of the three cruisers listed, the *Des Moines*-class cruisers designated for target, experimental use, or donation were scrapped. The vast majority of the World War II cruiser Navy ceased to exist by 1975 after sitting in reserve for years. A few vessels had just broken in their engines before being retired. The USS *Oregon City* (CA-122) was active for only 22 months of noncombat service, and sat in mothballs at the Philadelphia Naval Shipyard from December 15, 1947, until she was stricken on November 1, 1970. Likewise the USS *Fall River* (CA-131) was placed in reserve at Bremerton on October 31, 1947, and stricken on February 19, 1971.

Of the destroyer force, 131 out of 223 active *Gearing, Sumner,* and *Fletcher* (only three units) ships had been upgraded under FRAM from 1960 to 1964. Block obsolescence was temporarily deferred by the FRAM program; however, the ships were not intended to serve beyond 5 to 8 years after being modernized. Many were pressed into service for periods long beyond their maximum service life. Thirty ships were still active in 1975, which was 5 to 10 years longer than planned.

Of the remaining World War II–era destroyers in 1975, some were awaiting final disposition, and 54 had been acquired by foreign navies. The rest would soon be decommissioned and disposed of without serving an extensive period in the mothball fleet. There was no thought given to updating the typical World War II–built destroyer escorts (*Buckley, Evarts,* and *Rudderrow* classes), and they were scrapped or sold off.

Not all older U.S. Navy warships end their days in a boneyard or are scrapped. A few become museum ships, and many others are transferred to friendly foreign nations. The Brazilian *Gearing*-class destroyer *Mariz E. Barros* is the former USS *Brinkley Bass* (DD-887), which served from 1945 through 1975 in the U.S. Navy. The *Mariz E. Barros* was transferred in 1973, and had been upgraded with a FRAM refit that included an ASROC ASW weapon. Under Brazilian ownership, the World War II–era destroyer served into the mid-1990s. *Author's collection*

The year for massive reductions in the World War II fleet was 1975. Only three *Essex*-class aircraft carriers survived—the USS *Hancock* (CV-19) was sold for scrap on September 1, 1976, the USS *Oriskany* (CV-34) soldiered on until September 20, 1979, and the USS *Lexington* (CVT-16) was a training carrier through 1991. Overall, the U.S. Navy had 15 active carriers. That number had declined from 26 just a decade before, and there were 98 active carriers in 1945. The new foundation of the U.S. Navy's naval aviation strength was in its super carriers (e.g., USS *Forrestal* [CVA-59], USS *Enterprise* [CVN-65], and USS *Nimitz* [CVN-68]). Plans had been laid to build at least eight more huge nuclear-powered *Nimitz*-class (93,400 tons) aircraft carriers, and there was little comparison between that class and the 40,600-ton *Essex* class. None of the *Essex* class survived as front-line units after 1979.

Much of the World War II amphibious warfare and service force had been sold to foreign navies or broken up. The navies of Taiwan, South Korea, and Greece resembled mini American navies of the recent past because of the sheer numbers of former U.S. ships they possessed. A small number of the assembly-line built ships had been modified for modern purposes. Submarine tenders including the USS *Proteus* (AS-19) could be

The former USS *Proteus* is now identified as the IX-518 at the Suisun Bay Reserve Fleet anchorage in October 1999. The old tender had been refitted as an accommodation barge and had been assigned to the Puget Sound Naval Shipyard until she was brought down to Suisun Bay. From there she will likely be disposed of. *Author's collection*

This photo was taken on September 19, 1974, at West Waterway Lumber in Seattle, Washington. The *USNS SGT. Sylvester Antolak T-AP-192* (outboard) and *USNS PVT. Joe P. Martinez T-AP-187* (inboard) are in the last stages of being scrapped. Both have lost their propellers and the *Martinez* has been cut down below the main deck level. The cranes to the left are being used to lift pieces of the ships to awaiting rail cars or trucks to be taken to scrap metal dealers. *Courtesy L. Cote*

The *Charles F. Adams*-class guided missile destroyer USS *Claude V. Ricketts* (DDG-5) is shown at sea. This class of destroyers was well thought of in the Navy, but reached its performance limits in the late 1980s. The *Ricketts* and several of her sisters ended up at the inactive ship site in the Philadelphia Naval Shipyard. Others such as the USS *Hoel* (DDG-13) and USS *Henry B. Wilson* (DDG-7), were converted to mobile power barges at the Hunters Point Shipyard in San Francisco in the mid-1990s. *U.S.N.I.*

The former USS *Illusive* (MSO-448), an *Agile*-class ocean minesweeper, is being torn apart at Lambert Point in Baltimore, Maryland, by the Seawich Salvage Company. This September 20, 1993, photograph shows that much of the ship was made of wood as a safety measure when sweeping mines. Just across from the *Illusive*, the USS *Coral Sea* (CV-43) was also being broken up at the same time. The shipbreaking process is not a pretty sight. *U.S.N.I.*

The USS *Comte de Grasse* (DDG-974), a *Spruance*-class destroyer, is in mothballs at the Philadelphia Naval Shipyard in November 1999. This 24-year-old vessel had been decommissioned along with six others in the same class during a 1998 budget reduction action. The USS *Conolly* (DD-979) and USS *John Rodgers* (DD-983) were also in reserve at this site. All of the seven were retired because they were not armed with vertical missile launch capability. Twin arm launchers had become obsolete with the introduction of VLS. The *Comte de Grasse* will serve as logistic support (VLS) for the remaining *Spruance*-class destroyers. *Author's collection*

found in the backwaters of the mothball fleets, but they would soon be towed away and broken up.

By 1975, the die had been cast, and the end of the huge warship boneyards era was in sight. The active fleet had shrunk to 419 vessels, and at the end of 1976, it had 289 ships. There were 13 active aircraft carriers, 133 destroyer-type ships, and 74 attack submarines (SSN). The ballistic missile submarine force (SSBN), which was considered a strategic deterrent to Soviet attack, remained untouched at 41 boats. The fleet was being slowly modernized, but had only grown to 301 ships by late 1979. More than 1,300 World War II combat units had been disposed of by the end of the 1970s, leaving a legacy of fewer than 30 ships. The same was true of the National Defense Reserve Fleet (NDRF) of *Liberty*, *Victory*, and other World War II–built merchant ships. In

The *Leahy*-class guided missile cruiser, USS *Halsey* (CG-23), launches a missile from her forward twin-arm launch system. The *Halsey* was decommissioned due to budget cuts and the inability to compete with technologically updated ships (*Ticonderoga*-class CG). Her retirement date was in January 1994. *Author's collection*

This is "Cruiser row" at the Suisun Bay Reserve Fleet anchorage in October 1999. Nine *Belknap*- and *Leahy*-class guided missile cruisers are lined up to await disposal. All have been demilitarized. The USS *Halsey* (CG-23) is near the center showing its stern—sixth ship from the right (outboard of the transport *USNS General Edwin L. Patrick AP-124*). *Author's collection*

The aircraft carrier USS *Ranger* (CV-61) is moored in Bremerton, Washington, in this August 28, 1998, photograph. It was taken from the stern of the nuclear cruiser USS *California* (CGN-36), which was being formally inactivated. The *Ranger* has been at this facility since being decommissioned in 1993. In the background the USS *Midway* (CV-41) can be seen. *Author's collection*

The battleship USS *Iowa* (BB-61) is moored to the starboard side of the carrier USS *Saratoga* (CV-60) in November 1998. On the other side of the pier at the Newport, Rhode Island, facility is the first of the super carriers—the USS *Forrestal* (CV-59). In the 1980s, these ships and their escorts were the most powerful in the world. Now they await decisions as to their future—scrapyards or preservation? *Author's collection*

1970, there were 1,027 vessels moored in various locations, and 10 years later there were fewer than 300. As with excombat ships, most of the NDRF went to the shipbreakers.

Disposition of U.S. Naval Vessels through the Shipbreaking Process

The decision and process of selling a government-owned vessel for commercial use or scrapping is long and involved. It begins with a routine three-year review of each vessel held in reserve by a Navy Board of Survey and Review. The review determines a ship's value and continued suitability for military service. If it is decided that a vessel is no longer able to serve the fleet, a recommendation is made up through the Navy Department, ending with the Secretary of the Navy. If the secretary agrees with the board and all of the proper endorsements have been secured, then the vessel is stricken from the U.S. Naval Register on the first day of the month following. Ships can be transferred to friendly foreign powers, but during the 1970s, many were sold to commercial interests for scrapping. Former combatants, and those merchant vessels from the National Defense Reserve Fleet, were treated in much the same way

from this point onward. Ship dismantlers were notified of those ships being placed up for auction and told to make their bids in accordance with the particulars of the sale.

Vessels purchased were towed or pushed to shipbreaking locations on all coasts of the United States and in foreign countries such as Taiwan and India. Generally the scrapyards were located in the backwash of large harbors, where the hulks were moored alongside piers that had heavy-duty cranes designed to lift large bulk loads. In the 1970s warships were often sold

The USS *America* (CV-66) at the Philadelphia Naval Shipyard in November 1999. She was retired in late 1996 and has been cleared for sale to a shipbreaker in the year 2000. Behind the *America* is the USS *New Jersey* (BB-62), which has just arrived from Bremerton, Washington. The *New Jersey* was slated to be a museum ship in Camden, New Jersey, just across the river. *Author's collection*

to scrappers without first being demilitarized. It was the responsibility of the shipbreakers to destroy the weapons. Contemporary practice mandates that weapons are cut up prior to sale to private interests.

Breaking up a ship begins in a process opposite from its original construction. Using the ship's diagrams, the masts' antennae and upper superstructure are cut off and piled on the pier to await transport to storage areas or surplus metal dealers. Gun turrets, guns, lower superstructure, and interior compartments are cut up into manageable chunks and lifted onto the pier. Next, the interior machinery, engines, boilers, and ballast are removed down to the inner double hull of the ship. Many shipbreakers do not have the luxury or resources to place a hulk in drydock for the final process of chopping up a vessel, so a crude but effective alternative method is used. The aft part of the hull is ballasted with water to allow the bow to rise sufficiently to be dismantled and torn apart. The crane lifts the shell plating and frames

from the mud to the dock. The ship is then ballasted forward and the stern is cut up including the rudder and propeller, which are often torn loose by powerful tugs that are connected by cables. Finally, the remainder of the dismembered hulk is rammed up on the mud bank by tugs, and what is left after is pulled ashore by cables attached to bulldozers. This process is not a pretty sight, especially for veterans of the ship being dismantled who remember the former days of glory when their ship brought them home safely. To some, it is likened to old-style whaling, during which a thing of beauty became a carcass to be dismembered and rendered unidentifiable. The same degree of pomp and ceremony present at a warship's christening is absent at its end. By 1980, there were few reminders of the past, and the warship boneyards had far fewer occupants.

The methods used in the shipbreaking process unearthed certain major health and safety hazards. The revelations about the hazards of asbestosis and

The battle-scarred USS *Stark* (FFG-31) is in the inactive ship facility at the Philadelphia Naval Shipyard in November 1999. The *Stark* has been demilitarized and waits for disposition. Her history was different from all of her sisters in the *Oliver Hazard Perry* class. The frigate was patrolling in the center of the Persian Gulf on the night of May 17, 1987, when she was hit by two air-launched *Exocet* antiship missiles just forward of her bridge on the port side. An Iraqi *Mirage F-1* launched the missiles, and unfortunately the *Stark* did not have her defensive weapons on alert. The damage nearly sank the ship and killed 37 members of her crew. She survived due to superb damage control. *Author's collection*

Garcia-class *ASW* frigates USS *Voge* (FF-1047) (outboard) and USS *Edward McDonnell* (FF-1043) share a berth just ahead of the heavy cruiser USS *Des Moines* (CA-134) at the inactive ship site in the Philadelphia Naval Shipyard. The *Garcia* class was decommissioned in 1987 and 1988, and these two vessels show their age in this photograph. Both have been selected for future scrapping under a Naval Sea Systems Program. The *Voge* ran over a Soviet *Echo II* missile submarine on August 28, 1976, which sufficiently damaged it and required it to be towed. The *Echo II* survived, and was found at fault. *Author's collection*

other lethal illnesses inherent in this business compelled the government to crack down on careless operators. This had a depressing effect on the industry as a whole. The shipbreakers complained about intrusive government regulatory agencies that attempted to prevent chemical pollution and injury to workers. To the scrapper, this was a way of life, and it meant a wholesale change was necessary or else ships would remain idle until shipbreakers complied with environmental and public safety mandates.

Ronald Reagan's 600-Ship Navy

By the time Ronald Reagan was sworn in as president of the United States on January 20, 1981, the nation's armed forces had reached an all-time low in terms of its morale and its view of the future. The memory of the Vietnam War was still fresh, and four

years of the Jimmy Carter administration had done little to improve the force structure of the military and in particular, the U.S. Navy. Things would soon change.

On March 4, 1981, Secretary of Defense Casper Weinberger recommended increases in the defense budget of 11 percent in 1981 and 15 percent in 1982. A move that further stunned the public was the request to refit all four *Iowa*-class battleships for modern sea combat. There was some thought given to modernizing the heavy cruisers USS *Salem* (CA-139) and USS *Des* Moines (CA-134), but the durability of a battleship was needed to stand up to the new Soviet *Kirov*-class nuclear battle cruiser. Further recommendations were made to modernize the recently mothballed carrier USS *Oriskany* (CVA-34) and missile cruiser USS *Oklahoma City* (CLG-5), but nothing came of these.

The helicopter amphibious assault carriers USS *New Orleans* (LPH-11) (outboard) and USS *Okinawa* (LPH-3) are moored together at the end of a multi-ship row in Suisun Bay. They are members of the seven-ship *Iwo Jima* class that was commissioned from 1961 to 1970, and saw service in the Vietnam War. A third sister, the USS *Tripoli* (LPH-10) was tied up at Mare Island to wait disposal or sale at the time of this photograph in October 1999. *Author's collection by Carolyn Bonner*

The Reagan administration established a goal to have an active 600-warship navy. This was in reaction to the obvious fact that the U.S. Navy could not meet all of the required commitments. The Soviet Navy was steadily growing and improving, and by the year 2000, it might surpass the U.S. Navy as the most powerful in the world. Its ships sailed with impunity throughout the world's oceans and often uncomfortably close to the coastlines of United States and its allies. Escalating activity in the Persian Gulf and Indian Ocean mandated U.S. involvement to protect oil resources. Terrorism was becoming more common in the world and what had previously been a rarity in the Western world was on the increase. To checkmate these dangers, a large and well-balanced navy was needed to respond to multiple issues. The presence of a carrier battle group with a battleship at its center would give new meaning to the phrase "gunboat diplomacy."

The Navy stepped up new construction on the *Nimitz*-class nuclear carriers (CVN), *Ticonderoga*-class AEGIS cruisers (CG), *Oliver Hazard Perry*-frigates (FFG), *Los Angeles*-class-attack submarines (SSN) and *Ohio*-class ballistic missile boats (SSBN), but at the same time delayed the early retirement of

other vessels such as the two *Midway*-class aircraft carriers. The four *Iowa*-class battleships beginning with the USS *New Jersey* (BB-62) which was recommissioned on December 28, 1982, were refitted with modern electronics, 16 *Harpoon* antiship missiles, 32 *Tomahawk* cruise missiles, and 4 *Vulcan Phalanx* 20mm CIWS guns. Despite the sarcasm of their detractors, these four battleships were now the most powerful warships afloat.

The *Belknap*- and *Leahy*-class cruisers commissioned from 1962 to 1967 were upgraded, along with the nuclear cruisers USS *Long Beach* (CGN-9), USS *Bainbridge* (CGN-25), and USS *Truxton* (CGN-35). The *California*- and *Virginia*-class nuclear cruisers were also refitted and joined by 27-vessel *Ticonderoga* AEGIS-class cruisers. The *Charles F Adams*-class destroyers commissioned from 1960 to 1964 and the *Farragut* class (1959–1961) were joined by the four-ship *Kidd* class (1981–1982) and the popular *Spruance* (*Sprucan*) class (1975–1983). In 1985, the 29-ship *Arleigh Burke* class (DDG-51) of destroyers began to take shape.

The submarine force was augmented by the continued addition of *Los Angeles*-class nuclear attack boats and the ultimate ballistic missile submarine—the

114

Trident missile-armed *Ohio* class. Many of the older classes of nuclear attack boats, the *Permit, Skipjack,* and *Skate,* were kept active as were *Ethan Allen-* and *Lafayette*-class ballistic missile submarines. All of the five *Ethan Allen* SSBNs were converted to attack SSNs during the 1980s and reflected the critical need to counter Soviet submarine growth.

The 1980s was by all accounts a honeymoon period for the military and the Navy. The beginning of the end came in the late 1980s when it became apparent that the Soviet Navy was spending more time at anchor than at sea. The Soviet Union went into free fall in 1989 with the crumbling of the Berlin Wall in December of that year. The Soviet Navy was no longer viewed as a grave strategic threat.

The U.S. Navy now was the unchallenged leader at sea. With no significant blue-water enemy, it was obvious that the fleet had to shrink again. The warship boneyards that were occupied by the dregs of past wars now began to fill up again with surplus ships from the Cold War.

The "Peace Dividend" Warship Boneyard

The end of the Cold War produced the inevitable surplus of warships common at the conclusion of any major conflict. There were other factors at work as well. Many of the ships that sailed on in the 1980s were worn out and technologically obsolete. Ships that had been hard-wired

Three ships are moored at the Preble Avenue Wharf in the Philadelphia Naval Shipyard – November 1999. From left to right are the USS *San Diego* (AFS-6), USS *Boulder* (LST-1190) and USS *Kidd* (DDG-993). The 16,500-ton combat store ship *San Diego* served for 28 years and was decommissioned in late 1997. The *Boulder* was decommissioned in February 1994, and the *Kidd* stricken in March 1998. *Author's collection*

for automation were now obsolete thanks to the introduction of the microchip and personal computing power. *Harpoon* missiles and their launchers could not be adapted to some of the older destroyers due to space and weight constraints. This was a flashback to destroyer escorts 20 years earlier that were too small to accommodate updated weapons. Power plants that relied upon steam turbines, except the fleet carriers and nuclear submarines, were out of date. The propulsion plant of choice for nonnuclear warships was the gas turbine, and only the *Spruance* (DDG), *Kidd* (DDG), *Ticonderoga* (CG), and *Arleigh Burke* (DDG) classes of surface combatant were equipped with these turbines. This doomed the *Leahy* and *Belknap* classes of missile cruiser.

Crew requirements were examined and the ships found to be labor intensive were destined for the boneyard. In order to maintain a building program of modern multi-functional ships, the Navy was forced to retire scores of surface ships and submarines during the 1990s. It actually began in 1990 with the announcement that all 23 of the *Charles F Adams* DDGs and 11 *Farragut*-class DDGs would be retired over the following three years. Ten *Knox*-class frigates were also to be transferred to the Naval Reserve Force. A temporary respite occurred in late 1990 and early 1991 with the Persian Gulf War;

The USS *John Rodgers* (DD-983) (right) is moored next to the 1960s-era *Farragut*-class destroyer USS *Mahan* (DDG-42) at the Philadelphia Naval Shipyard inactive ship site in November 1999. The *Rodgers* was decommissioned and stricken in January 1998. The *Mahan* was sold to International Shipbreaking in Brownsville, Texas, on February 10, 1999. *Author's collection*

however, plans to retire ships on an accelerated basis continued unabated.

All of the *Iowa*-class battleships followed suit with the two *Midway*-class aircraft carriers, the USS *Midway* (CV-41) and USS *Coral Sea* (CV-43). In 1993 the original super carrier, the USS *Forrestal* (CV-59), which had been slated to assume the aviation training duties of the USS *Lexington* (CVT-16), was retired along with the USS *Ranger* (CV-61). In 1994, the USS *Saratoga* (CV-60) was decommissioned and placed in reserve, followed by the USS *America* (CV-66) in 1996. The *Lexington* ended up as a museum ship and the *Forrestal* and *Saratoga* reside at Newport, Rhode Island, where they are part of a training and education operation. The *Midway* and *Ranger* are warehoused at the Inactive Ship Maintenance Facility in Bremerton, Washington. In 1998, the USS *Independence* CV-62 was decommissioned and placed in reserve at Bremerton.

Of the remaining destroyers, the Navy began to retire *Spruance*-class destroyers that did not have the Vertical Launch System (VLS) for multi-functional missiles. The entire four-ship *Kidd*-class of antiair defense destroyers was decommissioned as were many of the *Knox* and *Oliver Hazard Perry* frigates. As of 2000, virtually all of the *Knox*-, *Garcia*-, and *Brooke*-class frigates were awaiting final disposition. The *Garcia* and *Brooke* classes

were among the first ships to be decommissioned in the late 1980s. A small number of *Oliver Hazard Perry* frigates were also awaiting sale to foreign bidders or the shipbreakers.

The amphibious, mine warfare, and service forces had not been spared the ax. Of the *Iwo Jima*-class (LPH) ships, all but the USS *Inchon* (MCS-12), which was converted to a mine countermeasure support ship and is now part of the Naval Reserve Force, were sent to the boneyard. All of the *Newport*-class LSTs have also been or are being decommissioned. The *Agile*-class ocean minesweepers have all been replaced by the 14-ship *Avenger* class of mine countermeasures ships (MCM). A few of the *Agile* class haunted inactive ship sites up through 2000. All will eventually be sold and broken up.

Recycling of Nuclear Submarines and Surface Ships

The process of disposing of nuclear warships is quite different than those that are fossil fueled. It is arduous, lengthy, and highly regulated at every step to prevent accidents. A heavily secured and well-guarded part of the Puget Sound Naval Shipyard has been established for the recycling effort, and there is a similar facility located at the Portsmouth Naval Shipyard in New Hampshire. Workers and visitors at the shipyards are required to view a film on safety issues before being allowed near the recycling area. The U.S. Navy has been disposing of its older nuclear submarines and all surface combatants since the early 1990s in the Nuclear Recycling Program.

By 1999, all of the nuclear cruisers (CGN) had been inactivated and their nuclear components removed. There have been 102 nuclear attack (SSN) and ballistic missile (SSBN) submarines processed through the Navy's nuclear recycling program at one of the two facilities. The process consists of the following major steps:

The nuclear warship (CGN, SSN, SSBN) is placed in a "standdown" status, preceded by a ceremony that formally lowers the steaming ensign. A skeleton crew is retained to help assist in the recycling process.

The nuclear fuel is then removed from the vessel through defueling of the nuclear reactor(s), and sent to Arco, Idaho, for reprocessing. They also de-energize and drain the systems and remove any reusable equipment.

This is the sail of the massive USS *Triton* (SSRN/SSN-586) at the Puget Sound Naval Shipyard on July 17, 1998. Built with multiple reactors, the 6,770-ton high-speed radar picket submarine was the largest submarine in the world when it was commissioned on August 19, 1958. The *Triton,* which circumnavigated the world in 1960 (voyage distance 41,519 miles over 84 days) is scheduled for recycling in 2004. The attack submarine USS *Lapon* (SSN-661) (right background) waits its turn to be recycled through the Navy's nuclear surface and submarine recycling program. *Author's collection*

The vessel is cut down to a hulk and then formally decommissioned and removed from the Naval Register. The Inactivation Ceremony takes place when the ship is still a viable unit. By the time the ship is decommissioned, only a nondescript hulk remains and very few people, if any, attend the brief ceremony.

The hulk and nuclear reactor components are cut up into manageable pieces. The reactor compartments are sent to Hanford, Washington, where they are placed in a deep trench. When the trench is full, the components will be buried. The steel (HY-80) used in the vessel's construction and other reusable metals are sold to commercial interests.

In 1999, the cost to recycle a nuclear attack submarine was $25.9 million; nuclear ballistic missile submarines cost $32 million, and nuclear cruisers $124.4 million. As of early 2000, there was a huge backlog of vessels awaiting disposition, and this is expected to continue for at least another 10 years. Several vessels have been sealed for the expected delay before being processed.

There has been some justifiable criticism of the Navy for its wholesale junking of the relatively modern *Virginia-* and *California*-class cruisers. The *California* had a minimum of 15 years of life left, which would have taken her to the year 2013. While she wasn't AEGIS or helicopter equipped, this cruiser and her sisters had value to the Navy. They could have saved the taxpayer millions of dollars in fossil fuel cost, which is expected to increase in the twenty-first century.

History repeats itself and this has been true for both the ships coming in and going out of the nation's warship boneyards. In the late 1970s, the Navy had all but eliminated its former World War II vessels from long-term storage in the reserve fleet. They had served the nation well in more than one crisis, and the decision to maintain them saved the taxpayers untold billions of dollars as well as ensured worldwide power protection by the United States. Taking the place of World War II ships were the ships from the same era that had been modernized, as well as other ships that had been built after the Korean War. These were then replaced by vessels that were built in the 1960s, 1970s, and 1980s. The warship boneyards were filled, emptied, and as of 1999 were full again. The budget axe and rampant technology were the twin culprits that seemed to precede a ship to a boneyard. Of course, this has been the case with the U.S. Navy since the beginning.

The USS Independence *(CV-62) entered the reserve fleet in September 1998. She was the last of the four-ship Forrestal-class super carrier to be inactivated. She is shown here at Bremerton after much of her supplies and fuel were removed. The 40-year-old carrier was refitted through a Service Life Extension Program (SLEP) in 1985 and will be retained in reserve. She will join the USS* Ranger *(CV-61) and the USS* Midway *(CVA-41) which are berthed at the other end of the naval base.* Author's collection

Chapter Ten
FUTURE OF THE WARSHIP BONEYARD

2000 AND BEYOND

The "Wild West days" of unregulated and poorly monitored ship-breaking were left behind in the mid-1990s. Environmental protection laws have been passed that define hazardous materials and how they have to be handled. Items such as asbestos, PCBs, and lead, whose previous long-term health effects were ignored, top the list of the most deadly substances to humans. Of course, regulation and strict compliance with environmental protection and worker safety rules cause sacrifice to the industry. According to the scrap metal industry, which prefers the title of "vessel recyclers," there is no profit when the government is intrusive. In the meantime, ships that should be

119

scrapped sit in National Defense Maritime Fleets or the U.S. Navy's Inactive Ship Maintenance sites. The money being spent to maintain and protect obsolete warships could be used for new construction or maintenance of active units.

In the 1990s, West Coast companies such as Pegasus Inc., Astoria Metals, and Southwest Marine attempted to make a profit from ship recycling. They soon discovered that warships contain large amounts of what is considered hazardous

material. In 1993, Southwest Marine took on the job of breaking up the former USS *Bon Homme Richard* (CV-31), an *Essex*-class aircraft carrier that was decommissioned on July 2, 1971. Ultimately, the shipbreaking effort cost more than was recovered from the sale of salvageable metals. The company recovered 50 tons of cable that had to be transported to another state for disposal due to a law prohibiting the disposal of hazardous material. The fees to transport the cable to another state

The USS *Barbel* (SS-580) lies like a dead whale against a pier owned by Southwest Marine in San Pedro, California, in October 1999. What was once a conventionally powered albacore-hull attack submarine was supposed to be dismantled, but the costs to finish the job exceeded any profits. The amount of asbestos in the boat was overwhelming. The *Barbel* was used as a set for the Disney film *Crimson Tide* and had a plywood sail built over the hole in the deck. Over the last several years, that has been the sum total of her accomplishments. The owners are currently stuck with the hulk. *Author's collection*

were enormous. Southwest Marine also acquired the USS *Barbel* (SS-580) and only partially dismantled the submarine before determining what the final costs would be. Again, the cost was more than could be gained from the sale of salvage-able metal.

Astoria Metals acquired the former USS *Hornet* (CVS-12) from the inactive fleet site in Bremerton, Washington, and in early 1995 the company was about to cut up the ship at Hunters Point in San Francisco when the vessel was purchased by a private foundation for public display. The shipbreaker was not sorry to lose the *Hornet* because of the exhorbitant costs to dismantle a 50-year-old ship full of asbestos and other hazardous materials.

Pegasus Inc., began breaking up the former USS *Oriskany* (CV-34), and just after the mainmast was cut down, the company filed for bankruptcy. The *Oriskany* sat at Mare Island until 1999 when she was towed to Beaumont, Texas, to await sale to another shipbreaker. Pegasus Inc. also defaulted on its contract to break up the catamaran-hulled subma-rine rescue vessels, USS *Pigeon* (ASR-21) and USS *Kiitawake* (ASR-13) as well as the amphibious ships, USS *Point Defiance* (LSD-31), USS *Thomaston* (LSD-28), and USS *Monticello* (LSD-35). The submarine rescue vessel and the amphibious craft had to be returned to the Suisun Bay Reserve Fleet for another form of disposal. The cost to taxpayers goes up whenever a ship has to reenter an inactive ship facility.

Several destroyers culled from East Coast reserve sites were purchased by Wilmington Resources Inc., a shipbreaker based in Wilmington, North Carolina, in the early 1990s. Nearly all of the ships were returned to the Philadelphia inactive fleet site in 1997 to be resold. Wilmington Resources Inc. had been closed by the state for violation of pollution laws.

Vessel scrapping has become an international political and environmental scandal. Reduced demands for recycled metals, as well as other diffi-culties, have drastically decreased the number of scrap yards. Labor costs have skyrocketed in most domestic shipyards, and environmental pressures have caused a near stoppage of scrapping in the

Posing as a mock-up of the *Ohio*-class ballistic missle submarine the USS *Alabama* (SSBN-731) for the film *Crimson Tide*, the USS *Barbel* (SS-580) assumes a new mission as a backdrop for the film's pierside shots. Originally commissioned in 1959, the *Barbel* was the lead boat of a three-ship class of advanced diesel electrics, and one of the first to use the advanced teardrop Albacore hull. *Author's collection*

United States. This has caused the Navy to look to foreign countries for ship disposal. However, that alternative has been severely criticized after the media exposed terrible shipbreaking practices in Alang, India, where several ex–Soviet navy ships and the former *Essex*-class USS *Bennington* (CVS-20) met their end. Photos taken at Alang in 1995 showing women and children cutting up carriers with Stone Age tools for less than $1 a day were dev-astating for the continued use of foreign scrappers.

With current international attention drawn to the unhealthy and dangerous practices of contemporary shipbreaking, the illegal dumping of ships or improper and clandestine shipbreaking are becoming more prevalent. Booming scrapyards in Alang, India; Pakistan; Taiwan; La Spezia, Italy; and others are being monitored by watchdog organizations such as Greenpeace International until some form of safety regulations can be agreed to and adopted. Warships from the Soviet Union and Western powers and Allies still find their way to the beaches of India and Pakistan to be dismantled.

Most ship recycling firms have requested the Navy consider a revision in its method of selling fossil fuel ships for disposal. Citing the example of the high costs to recycle a nuclear-powered vessel, the shipbreaking industry has petitioned for a cost-plus contract to dispose of former warships. The Navy has also been criticized for selling ships to foreign shipbreakers where there are no realistic safety controls. Greenpeace International is closely monitoring shipbreaking sites around the world to determine if the industrialized nations of the West are using Third World countries as dumping grounds for excess ships. The remains of the aircraft carrier USS *Bennington* (CVS-20) were sighted at Alang, India, being broken up by women and children with crude tools in the late 1990s. The photographs of the rusting hulk being clamored over by children caused a worldwide media outcry. Due to adverse publicity, this method of ship disposal has been suspended. There was some thought given to refurbishing decommissioned combat vessel power plants for domestic electric generation. Consolidated Minerals Inc. of northern California attempted to inaugurate something similar with the rebuilt *Charles F. Adams* destroyers USS *Hoel* (DDG-13) and USS *Henry B. Wilson* (DDG-7), but was unsuccessful. The vessels were returned to the Suisun Bay Reserve Fleet.

The USS *C. Turner Joy* (DD-951) sits in Bremerton, Washington, as a museum ship. The *Turner Joy* was brought out of the mothball fleet at Bremerton and restored to her likeness when she and the USS *Maddox* (DD-731) entered the Tonkin Gulf in August 1964. What followed was the Tonkin Gulf Resolution and the escalation of the Vietnam War. The *Turner Joy* and a handful of other vessels dot the harbors of the United States and serve to remind the public of the Navy's role in keeping the United States safe. *Author's collection*

This is a bow shot of the USS *Claude V. Ricketts* (DDG-5) as she sits at the Philadelphia Naval Shipyard in November 1999. She has already been partially cut up by Wilmington Resources Inc., a shipbreaker that was sanctioned by the state. The *Ricketts* was returned to the inactive fleet site with several other ships that were to be scrapped. This image of the once-great ship that did so much during the Cold War is sad, but reflects what a warship boneyard is truly like. *Author's collection*

Some vessels that escape scrapping or simple storage are donated to other government agencies, such as the Coast Guard, or to Merchant Marine academies for use as school ships. The former surveying ship USNS *Maury* (AGS) became the training ship *Golden Bear* for the California Maritime Academy in 1998.

The ship donation program was capable of absorbing only a small percentage of those vessels up for disposal, and thus the inactive fleet sites become crowded. In response to the problem of contemporary shipbreaking, the Navy agreed to begin a pilot program with four destroyers in September 1999. Under strict EPA/Navy supervision, four separate ship recyclers were alotted a *Knox*-class frigate for disposal. As of mid-2000, the USS *Patterson* (FF-1061), USS *Blakely* (FF-1072), USS *Lockwood* (FF-1064), and USS *Bagley* (FF-1069) were successfully and safely broken up. This pilot project has been extended and may break the logjam of ships that wait for disposal. Contracts were to be let on a cost-plus basis for recycling the ships. This was the only viable alternative left to solve the problem of an overage of ships crowding inactive fleet sites. Only the ships that may be of some use in the future will be retained.

The Future of Warship Boneyards

The high point of the twentieth-century warship boneyard was reached just after World War II (1946–1950). It is likely that the U.S. Navy or any navy in the world will never again retire and maintain 2,000 ships in reserve. The U.S. Navy of the twenty-first century will be greatly reduced in ship numbers, yet more powerful than any force previously sent to sea. The microchip, missile, and leapfrogging technology have made single ships, such as the *Arleigh Burke* destroyers, as potent as an entire squadron of World War II destroyers. Unfortunately, a few ships cannot police the entire world, and crises are not always sequential—they often occur simultaneously.

Ships placed in reserve today will not likely remain so for 20 years as did those from World War II. Ships that are inactivated in the future will be technologically inferior and not reuseable at a later date. Everything that can be done to upgrade existing warships will be done to forestall inactivity. A

50-year lifespan for a warship should become common. For nuclear aircraft carriers, the length of service is basically standard. The U.S. Navy will operate with fewer combat vessels, and there will not be a need for extensive inactive fleet sites. The warship boneyard will become a place of transition for a vessel moving from decommissioning to another status. Ships that will occupy the inactive fleet sites on a routine basis will be those that are required periodically—similar to the current ready reserve fleet or pre-positioning ships. The need to store this type of vessel is not expected to disappear in the near future. Visitors to America's warship boneyards will still see rows of ships but it will never be on the scale of that in the mid-twentieth century. In Bremerton, Washington, and Suisun Bay, California, there are vista points for visitors who want a closer look. There is also an anchor with a plaque near the Inactive Ship Maintenance Facility in Bremerton—it commemorates the four *Iowa*-class battleships USS *Iowa,* USS *New Jersey,* USS *Missouri,* and USS *Wisconsin.* These ships have risen to be among the most honored warships in the world, and the movement to preserve them has become important to our heritage. Without 50 years of U.S. Navy preservation in one warship boneyard or another, these mighty ships would no longer exist.

During the years since 1900, the world has been in a virtual state of continuous warfare, and consequently there was a need for strong navies. At the halfway point of the century, there were thousands of warships serving in the combined navies of the world. At the turn of the twenty-first century, the navies of the world are much smaller. The U.S. Navy has 327 warships of all types and less than 60 submarines. Today the Navy is the most powerful seaborne force in the world and has adopted responsibilities that were inconceivable 100 years ago.

It is certain that the magnitude of twentieth-century warship boneyards will never be seen again. It was truly a passing phenomenon. People from around the world came to look at the major reserve fleet sites. The number of warships from World War II and the conflicts that followed will continue to decline, and contemporary warships will likely be laid up in reserve, but in numbers that will be insignificant to the past. The only reminder of the massive boneyards will be the surviving ships that became museums or memorials. The age of the crowded warship boneyard is rapidly passing into history.

The warship boneyards of the twentieth century were wonders of naval might that have, or soon will, all but disappear forever—fortunately, we have reminders in those ships that were preserved and saved.

The former ocean escort USS *Lockwood* (FF-1064) lies alongside a pier at the Hunters Point Shipyard in San Francisco, California, on April 16, 2000. This *Knox*-class frigate, along with three other sisters, USS *Bagley* (FF-1069), USS *Blakely* (FF-1072), and USS *Patterson* (FF-1061), are part of a pilot project to recycle former warships using environmentally-safe methods and improved worker safety. The shipbreaking jobs are done on a cost-plus basis. The *Patterson* and *Blakely* are being processed in East Coast yards, and the *Bagley* is in Brownsville, Texas. If the pilot project is successful and not expensive, it will be employed to dispose of scores of older warships sitting in boneyards around the United States. *Author's collection*

BIBLIOGRAPHY

Primary Materials

Private Papers–Manuscript/Photo Files

Belford, Middlebrook, and Company–The American Navy, Photographs, 1898.

Bisharat, George; Photo collection.

Bonner, Kermit H.; Private papers and photo collection.

Burgess, Richard; Navy League Photo Files (Soviet Navy).

Call Bulletin Newspaper File, 1994, Treasure Island Museum.

Cote, Larry; Private papers and photo collection.

Greenpeace International.

Southwest Marine.

Special Collections–Manuscripts/Photo Collections.

Suisun Bay Reserve Fleet.

Treasure Island Museum Photo Files, 1994–Various.

U.S. Naval Institute, 1997, 1998, 1999–Various.

U.S. Navy–CHINFO, Office of Information, 1999–Various.

Vallejo Naval and Historical Museum.

Interviews

Baker, John; USS *Oklahoma City* Association, August 1999.

Burgess, Richard; Managing Editor, Sea Power, Navy League–Various 1998, 1999.

Cavas, Chris; Naval Historian and Photo Journalist–Various 1999.

Clayton, Pete, and Bob Rogers; USS *Hornet* Foundation, August 1999.

Currie, Dick; SS *Jeremiah O'Brien* Association, January 2000.

Flaherty, Joe and Staff; Inactive Ship Maintenance Facility, Philadelphia Naval Shipyard, November 1999.

Goite, Joe; Naval Sea Systems Command, October 1999.

Grey, Mike; *Baltimore Sun*, July 1999.

Johnson, David; Center for Defense Information, Washington, D.C., February 1999.

Lee, Jeff; Southwest Marine Corporation, October 1999.

Naval Inactive ship facility, Bremerton, Washington, Pete Galassi, Bob Callaghan, August 1999.

Peccoraro, Joe; Suisun Bay Reserve Fleet, October 1999.

Public Affairs Office, Puget Sound Naval Shipyard, Bremerton, Washington, August 1998.

Smookler, Angela, Public Affairs Officer; Naval Sea Systems Command, September 1999.

Swank, John, Public Affairs Officer; Maritime Administration, December 1999.

U.S. Navy Cruiser Sailors Association, Edward August–Various 1998.

U.S. Government Documents

Department of Defense, Defense Supply Agency, Sealed Bid–Heavy Cruiser Ex-CA-135 and Guided Missile Cruiser Ex-CLG-3, 4/30/1975.

Department of the Navy, *Naval Sea Systems Command, Naval Ships Technical Manual S9086-BS-STM-000*, Chapter 50, Rev. 1991.

Naval Sea Systems Command, Guide to NISMF, Philadelphia–1999.

NISMF, Philadelphia, Ship Disposal Status–1999.

U.S. Government Printing Office, *Dictionary of American Naval Fighting Ships*, Volume V, 1979.

U.S. Maritime Administration, Guide to Suisun Bay Reserve Fleet–1999.

Secondary Materials

Books, Monographs, Treaties

Blackman, Paul, *The World's Warships*, Hanover House, 1960.

Blackman, Raymond, V. B. *Jane's Fighting Ships 1968-1969*, BPC Publishing, Ltd., 1969.

Bonner, Kit and Carolyn, *Cold War at Sea,* MBI Publishing Company, 2000.

Bonner, Kit and Carolyn, *Great Naval Disasters*, MBI Publishing Company, 1998.

Bonner, Kit, *Final Voyages*, Turner Publishing, 1999.

English, Adrian, *Armed Forces of Latin America*, Jane's Publishing Co. Ltd., 1984.

Faulkner, Keith, *Jane's Warship Recognition Guide*, Harper Collins Publishing, 1996.

Friedman, Norman, *Modern Warship Design and Development*, Mayflower Books, 1979.

Friedman, Norman, *U.S. Cruisers*, Naval Institute Press, 1984.

Friedman, Norman, *U.S. Destroyers*, Naval Institute Press, 1982.

Humble, Richard, *Submarines, The Illustrated History*, Basinghall Books Ltd., 1981.

Jane's Publishing, *Jane's Fighting Ships,* 1919-1920, 1940-41,1945–6, 1948, 1950–51, 1960–61, 1968–69, 1975, 1987–88, 1996–97.

Jane's Publishing, *Jane's Warship Recognition Guide,* 1996.

Jordan, John, *Modern U.S. Navy,* Prentice Hall Press, 1986.

Madsen, Daniel, *Forgotten Fleet, The Mothball Navy*, Naval Institute Press, 1999.

McNeil, Jim, *Charleston's Navy Yard,* Cokercraft Press, 1985.

Mickel, Peter, Hansgeorg Jentschura, and Dieter Jung, *Warships of the Imperial Japanese Navy, 1869–1945*, Naval Institute Press, 1977.

Moineville, Hubert, *Naval Warfare Today and Tomorrow,* Basil Blackwell Publishing, 1983.

Moore, Capt. R. N. John, *Jane's American Fighting Ships of the 20th Century,* Mallard Press, 1991.

Morison, Samuel Eliot, *History of the United States Naval Operations in World War II,* Vol. XV, Atlantic-Little Brown, 1962.

Muir, Malcolm Jr., *Black Shoes and Blue Water,* Naval Historical Center, 1996.

Palmer, Michael, *On Course to Desert Storm, The United States Navy and the Persian Gulf,* Naval Historical Center, 1992.

Polmar, Norman, *Chronology of the Cold War at Sea,* Naval Institute Press, 1998.

Preston, Anthony, *Warships of the World,* Jane's Publishing, 1980.

Roger C., *Spy Sub*, Penguin Books, 1996.

Schofield, Capt. USNR William G., *Destroyers–60 Years,* Rand McNally & Company, 1962.

Silverstone, Paul, *U.S. Navy 1945 to the Present,* Arms and Armour Press, 1991.

Silverstone, Paul, *U.S. Warships Since 1945,* Naval Institute Press, 1987.

Sommervile, Donald, *World War II Day by Day,* Dorset Press, 1989.

Sultzberger, C. L., *The American Heritage Picture History of World War II*, Crown Publishers, 1966.

Sweetman, Jack, *American Naval History,* Naval Institute Press, 1984.

Tazewell, William, *Newport News Shipbuilding, The First Century,* The Mariners Museum, 1986.

Terzibaschitsch, Stephan, *Aircraft Carriers of the U.S. Navy,* Naval Institute Press, 1978.

Watts, Anthony, *Axis Submarines,* Arco Publishing Co., 1997.

Wright & Logan, *The Royal Navy in Focus 1960–69,* Maritime Books, 1981.

Articles

Alden, Cmdr. (Ret.) USN John D., *Tomorrow's Fleet, Naval Institute Proceedings,* January 1981.

Baldwin, Hanson, "New Jobs for Old Ships," *Naval Institute Proceedings,* June 1958.

Bonner, Kit, "The End of an Era, The USS *Oklahoma* CLG-5 Departs on Her Final Cruise," *U.S. Navy Cruiser Sailors Association,* Spring, 1999.

Bonner, Kit, *Tonkin Gulf Incident,* Sea Classics, Spring 1995.

Brown, Lt. Cmdr. USNR Gordon, "Sea Power in Reserve," *Naval Institute Proceedings,* June 1967.

Bunker, John, "Tribute to the Liberties," *Naval Institute Proceedings,* March 1960.

Buxton, II, "Breaking Up HM Ships," *Warship,* 1982.

Chaplin, Phillip, "The Reincarnation of the Four-stackers," *Naval Institute Proceedings,* March 1960.

Clark, Cmdr. USNR Ellery, "New Ships and Conversions–1945–1955," *Naval Institute Proceedings,* March, 1956.

Degnan, Lt. (jg) USN James L., *Oiler Parade,* September 1958.

Degnan, Lt. (jg) USN James L., "The Clermont and the Beginnings of Steam," *Naval Institute Proceedings,* August 1957.

Englund, Will and Gary Cohn, "Scrapping Ships, Sacrificing Men," *The Sun,* December 7, 1997.

Fredeen, Mel, "Scrapping Our World War II Navy," *Naval Institute Proceedings,* February 1979.

Friedman, Norman, "World Naval Developments," *Naval Institute Proceedings,* June 1993.

Friedman, Norman, "World Navies in Review," *Naval Institute Proceedings,* March 1994.

Gray, Thomas, "New Roles for Old LST's," *Naval Institute Proceedings,* December 1965.

Hanford, Franklin, Rear Admiral, "How I Entered the Navy," *Naval Institute Proceedings,* June 1965.

Hessler, William H., "There's No Substitute for Diplomacy or Power," *Naval Institute Proceedings,* July 1957.

Howe, Walter Bruce, "Why the United States Should Maintain a Full Strength Treaty Navy," *Naval Institute Proceedings,* October 1929.

Hussman, Cmdr. USN H. L., "Inactivation of the *Randolph,*" *Naval Institute Proceedings,* November 1969.

Kassel, Lt. Cmdr. USN Bernard M., "The Lend Lease Fleet,*" Naval Institute Proceedings,* May 1952.

Kersting, Lt. USN W. H., "The Selected Reserve-Problem in Readiness," January 1964.

King, Capt. USMM Thomas, "Ships of the National Defense Reserve Fleet Sail Again," *Naval Institute Proceedings,* August 1968.

Kirk, Neville, "The Navy Gets Its First Reserve," *Naval Institute Proceedings,* June 1955.

Marx, Hans, "The United States Merchant Marine," *Naval Institute Proceedings,* December 1963.

McDonald, Capt. USN Edwin A., "Bellingshausen Sea Operation," *Naval Institute Proceedings,* September 1960.

Moon, Lt. Cmdr USN D. P., "Recommissioning the Destroyers," *Naval Institute Proceedings,* February 1931.

Morison, Samuel L., "Changes in U.S. Naval Forces, January 1, 1998–December 31, 1998," *Naval Institute Proceedings,* May 1999.

Nelson, Charles, Chief Journalist, USN, "Puget Sound–the Navy's New Frontier," *Naval Institute Proceedings,* November 1963.

Oliver, Capt. USCG Edward F., Capt., "A Chain of Ships," *Naval Institute Proceedings,* November 1969.

Palazzolo, Lt. Cmdr. USN Anthony, "Growler Sea Trials," *Naval Institute Proceedings,* July 1960.

Polmar, Norman, "The U.S. Navy Frigates," *Naval Institute Proceedings,* July 1980.

Sibley, John, "126th Ship Leaves Mothball Fleet for Vietnam Service," *The New York Times,* July 17, 1966 (reprint in *U.S. Naval Institute Proceedings,* October 1966).

Sloan, Edward, III, "Isherwood's Masterpiece," *Naval Institute Proceedings,* December 1965.

Smelser, Marshall, "Whether to Provide and Maintain a Navy (1787–1788)," *Naval Institute Proceedings,* September 1957.

Staff Written, "38 Ships Returned to Reserve Status," *Naval Institute Proceedings,* May 1969.

Staff Written, "Back to the Wars," *Naval Institute Proceedings,* October 1967.

Staff Written, "Bringing Back the Battleship," *Warship International,* March 1983.

Staff Written, "Carrier Will be Electronics Lab," *Naval Institute Proceedings,* September 1965.

Staff Written, "Desert Shield, The Forces," *Naval Institute Proceedings,* January 1991.

Staff Written, "First of World War II *Essex* Class Axed," *Naval Institute Proceedings,* March 1965.

Staff Written, "Imperial Japanese Navy Boneyard," *All Hands,* December 1945.

Staff Written, "Liberty Ships Up for Bids," *Naval Institute Proceedings,* March 1964.

Staff Written, "Naval Forces Summary, February 1979," *Naval Institute Proceedings,* May 1979.

Staff Written, "Ship Notes–United States," *Naval Institute Proceedings,* July 1964.

Staff Written, "Ship Notes–United States," *Naval Institute Proceedings,* November 1965.

Staff Written, "Sub Savvy," *All Hands,* July 1947.

Staff Written, "Summary of Major Military Forces, January 1980," *Naval Institute Proceedings,*" May 1980.

Staff Written, "The Destroyer," *Life,* February 24, 1941.

Staff Written, "U.S. Naval Battle Force Changes, January–December 1997" *Naval Institute Proceedings,* May 1998.

Staff Written, "U.S. Submarine Base New London," *Naval Institute Proceedings,* February 1958.

Staff Written, *Sea Power,* 1990, 1991, 1992, 1993, 1994, 1995, 1996, 1997, 1998, 1999, 2000 issues, Navy League of the United States.

Sternlicht, Lt. (jg) USNR Sanford, "Ninety-nine Years in the Navy," *Naval Institute Proceedings,* May 1959.

Switzer, Harold E., "The Mothball Fleet," *Naval Institute Proceedings,* April, 1965.

Van Deurs, Rear Admiral (Ret.) USNG, "A Naval Pioneer on Puget Sound," *Naval Institute Proceedings,* November 1957.

Votaw, Homer, "The *Independence,* Our First Ship of the Line," *Naval Institute Proceedings,* April 1958.

White, Lt. Cmdr. (SC) George, USN, "Maladie de Paix," *Naval Institute Proceedings,* September 1965.

White, William L., "Atlantic Crossing on U.S. Destroyer," *Life,* December 2, 1940.

Whitehurst, Clinton, "The National Reserve Fleet: Past, Present and Future," *Naval Institute Proceedings,* February 1977.

Wright, Christopher, "*Albany* (CG-10) and *Chicago* (CG-11) Leave the Active Fleet," *Warship International,* March, 1983.

INDEX